Get Set for Sociology

Titles in the GET SET FOR UNIVERSITY series:

Get Set for American Studies
ISBN 0 7486 1692 6

*Get Set for Communication
 Studies*
ISBN 0 7486 2029 X

Get Set for Computer Science
ISBN 0 7486 2167 9

Get Set for English Language
ISBN 0 7486 1544 X

Get Set for English Literature
ISBN 0 7486 1537 7

Get Set for History
ISBN 0 7486 2031 1

*Get Set for Media & Cultural
 Studies*
ISBN 0 7486 1695 0

Get Set for Nursing
ISBN 0 7486 1956 9

Get Set for Philosophy
ISBN 0 7486 1657 8

Get Set for Politics
ISBN 0 7486 1545 8

Get Set for Psychology
ISBN 0 7486 2096 6

Get Set for Sociology
ISBN 0 7486 2019 2

Get Set for Study in the UK
ISBN 0 7486 1810 4

Get Set for Teacher Training
ISBN 0 7486 2139 3

Get Set for Sociology

Ian McIntosh and Samantha Punch

Edinburgh University Press

© Ian McIntosh and Samantha Punch, 2005

Edinburgh University Press Ltd
22 George Square, Edinburgh

Typeset in Sabon
by Hewer Text Ltd, Edinburgh, and
Printed and bound in Finland by WS Bookwell

A CIP record for this book is
available from the British Library

ISBN 0 7486 2019 2 (paperback)

CONTENTS

ACKNOWLEDGEMENTS

Thanks to Sarah Edwards at Edinburgh University Press and to our friends and colleagues in the Department of Applied Social Science at Stirling University, in particular Jacqueline Davidson, Douglas Robertson and Ruth Emond for their helpful suggestions and general banter. Thanks are also due to the tutors and students at Stirling who took the time to comment on various draft chapters. This book is dedicated to students, past and present, at Stirling University; teaching on the first-year undergraduate courses has enabled us to write and reflect on much of the material we present here.

PART I
Choosing Sociology

1 INTRODUCTION

Academic fashions come and go but sociology remains a popular choice for a first degree and has done so for a considerable time. Clearly, this comes as no surprise to us but what exactly is sociology? A common (perhaps the most common) answer to this question is that it is the 'study of society' or the 'social world'. This may be on the glib side but at least it is indicative of the breadth of interests of sociologists; every facet of social life is a potential, or actual, topic for study. This encompasses large-scale social issues down to the most minute details of social life. Thus the smoking habits of women in the UK or a study of social interaction in a nightclub are valid subjects for the intrepid sociologist. In general, sociologists focus on problematic areas of the social world, the ways in which societies are divided and issues to do with social change. The ways in which these issues are theorised and practically investigated form the bulk of Parts II and III of this text, so read on if you want further clarification!

Presumably the hope of most of those studying sociology is that they will reach a clearer understanding of society, in all its complexities. Of course, sociology can never hope to 'explain' completely the social world but it does have the great merit of generally acknowledging that the world is a complicated place. Thus, even if we do not get satisfactory answers, we can at least pose some interesting and valuable questions. Given this, it is little wonder that people are intrigued by sociology and the promise it holds out for providing a better understanding of the complex, and at times bewildering, world that we are immersed in. Sociology then is a discipline that resonates with many people of all ages and backgrounds. This book aims to introduce you to some of the central concerns and approaches of sociologists. Hopefully we can clue you in as to what is distinctive about a sociological approach and prepare you for your journey through your sociology studies at university.

Most of you reading this text will have recently left school, which is why we sometimes refer to the differences between what is expected at university and school. We also recognise that some of you will be mature students who are returning to study after several years. This book is aimed at you both, and we try to deal with most of the fears and questions you may have in relation to studying sociology at university. To this end Part IV is devoted to outlining the study skills that you can develop and work on to get the most from doing your degree in sociology.

In order to engage your interest, we have written the book in a fairly informal style. Bear in mind that when you write your own sociological essays you will need to adopt a more formal academic tone, so do as we say but not as we do! We assume that the reader has no prior knowledge of sociology but, if we attempted to explain everything at every turn, we would end up with several large volumes instead of the slim single text you have in your hand. University should be a challenging experience that stretches you intellectually, so you will come across some 'intimidating' words, terms and concepts that you will not be familiar with and which you may not understand immediately. You should get used to not 'getting' everything first time and realise that you will have to work at developing your sociological knowledge gradually, so be patient with yourself. One of the excellent sociology dictionaries on the market can be very helpful in this respect and we have provided a glossary to help clarify the meaning of some key concepts and terms you will come across.

Our intention is that you consult this book prior to going to university to give you a flavour of what to expect from, and how to approach, your studies in sociology. We also hope that you will continue to find it a useful and interesting text during your encounters with the many and varied delights of sociology.

2 WHY STUDY SOCIOLOGY?

Some of us study sociology for its own sake, finding it a fascinating intellectual challenge and providing us with new perspectives on the social world. Since sociology is often concerned with contemporary social issues, such as family problems, crime, drug use and poverty, many people find it inherently interesting as it deals with topics that surround their everyday lives. Others do it because it complements other courses, social policy, criminology, philosophy, psychology or social work, for example. The best reason for doing sociology is because you find it interesting and revelatory, but it does bring with it transferable skills – bonuses which often go unrecognised and which can be of lifelong benefit to you. So, before we look more closely at the subject matter of sociology we will run through some of the skills that can accrue from your degree, both those of a general nature and those more specific to sociology.

GENERAL TRANSFERABLE SKILLS

Why are you going to university? You may be a seeker of knowledge and/or you may be going for the social life and/or you may be going because it is expected of you. Whatever your reasons, graduation day comes around sooner than you think and you may then be looking for a job. You would expect a university degree to improve your job prospects, but have you ever wondered why? If you become a teacher or a social researcher, then sociological knowledge may well be the main focus of your employment. However, there are a much wider range of jobs which a sociology graduate can undertake.

Thus, in addition to the knowledge you have accumulated

through your course you will have developed a range of 'transferable skills' that are useful for many occupations. At university you can improve on the basic academic skills of literacy and numeracy. Information technology and library skills will also be enhanced (see Chapter 11). In addition, you can engage in independent learning and develop the ability to work by yourself. Furthermore, in workshops you can learn how to work as part of a group (see Chapter 13) as well as develop both your written and oral communication skills. Perhaps the most general skills that any university graduate will develop are those relating to motivation and self-management (see Chapter 10).

SELF-MANAGEMENT SKILLS

- Self-motivation

- Time management

- Working under pressure

- Meeting deadlines

- Planning and organisation

University students have to learn to apply a range of study skills and the first they must foster is the ability to work on their own. Self-motivation is not easy as there are often many distractions at university which can take you away from your studies. This is not always a bad thing but successfully completing a degree does involve an ability to assign your own manageable goals and work towards them by setting priorities, keeping to deadlines and managing your time effectively. Organising your academic workload sensibly can be crucial when you may also be trying to juggle part-time employment and other activities.

During your university experience, you should also try to

develop the ability to learn from your mistakes by critically reflecting on any weaknesses. Building up stamina to keep persevering with what can be difficult intellectual tasks is also an ability worth developing. Ultimately you should aim to take responsibility for much of your own learning and actively seek the additional help as and when you need it. This may involve you in developing library and computer skills, or a more sophisticated writing style or particular presentation skills. These planning and organisational skills may also be useful for running your life!

SOCIOLOGY'S TRANSFERABLE SKILLS

In addition to the general transferable skills that you gain during your degree, sociology allows you to develop a useful range of academic and communication skills and can help you become self-aware (note that by this we do not mean self-conscious) and reflexive.

ACADEMIC SKILLS

Reading: Sociology can enhance reading skills (see Chapter 11). This in turn can help you to analyse different kinds of texts and make sense of often difficult ideas. In particular, you can develop your critical abilities by questioning what you read and not taking information at face value but scrutinising it and challenging any taken-for-granted assumptions. For example, you may become more critical of the media as a reliable source of information. You will also be able to improve your note-taking and summarising skills whilst learning to manage and organise large amounts of information.

Critical and analytical thought: It is to the great credit of sociology that it is a subject that can enhance your ability to think critically. In time you will be expected to think clearly, critically and logically as well as seek out and evaluate evidence for any claims you make. Furthermore, presenting your own balanced arguments can allow you to consider different perspectives, highlighting both the positive and negative aspects of various viewpoints.

Referencing: When writing at university you should get used to backing up your ideas with reliable evidence. In order to substantiate the points you make the skills of referencing and providing a proper bibliography are important techniques to learn (see section on 'Referencing' in Chapter 14).

Research skills: Studying sociology can help you trace information from a variety of sources and then be critical about its content. Thereby you learn to identify relevant material and be selective about the evidence you employ. Problem-solving skills can be developed through regular analysis of empirical case studies and this will allow you to create strategies to deal with key issues that arise. In the later years of your sociology degree you are likely to have an opportunity to write a dissertation by conducting some of your own research. By then you will almost certainly have received training in social research methods and data analysis which you can then put into practice.

COMMUNICATION SKILLS

Writing: Sociology can improve your written communication skills, helping you to write concisely, accurately and unambiguously. When writing sociological essays you will learn how to present information, develop an argument and answer the question succinctly without straying away from the central issues (see Chapter 14). You should then be able to develop your own writing style and to articulate both your own and other people's ideas in a clear and logical manner. Essay writing can give you an ability to pay close attention to detail, as well as encourage you to work to word limits and meet deadlines – of which you will encounter many!

Speaking: Workshops should help to develop your verbal communication skills and give you the confidence to speak in front of others. Ideally they can provide a supportive context within which you can learn to articulate your ideas clearly. Making class presentations involves planning and preparation and can give you the opportunity to become adept in the use of audiovisual aids.

Group work: During workshops you are also likely to be given opportunities for team working through project work carried out in groups. Working as part of a team is a valuable (if at times frustrating) experience as it can help you get the most out of yourself and others, share knowledge and improve your skills of negotiation, not to mention tact!

SELF-AWARENESS AND REFLEXIVITY

The heart of sociology is about the interpretation and critical analysis of social life. Bauman and May highlight how sociology can act as a means for 'refining the knowledge we possess and employ in our daily life' (2001: 166). They suggest that this can bring into focus:

> not only our achievements, but also the constraints and possibilities we face by connecting our actions to the positions and conditions in which we find ourselves. Sociology is a disciplined eye that both examines 'how' we get on in our daily lives, and locates those details onto a 'map' that extends beyond those immediate experiences. (Bauman and May 2001: 166)

Sociology enables us, then, to develop self-awareness and self-understanding, facilitating an increased recognition of what enables and constrains our, and others', actions. So sociology can make us more reflexive: an ability to critically assess and reassess our thoughts and actions.

INTERPERSONAL SKILLS

A sociological understanding of the world is not only of benefit to us when reflecting on our own individual life trajectories but it also enables us to consider how our lives are intertwined with others. This enhances our ability to see the world from other viewpoints and to engage with people from different backgrounds. It encourages us to become more tolerant and sensitive to cultural differences, also increasing our ability to read non-verbal signs and take into account other people's feelings. Interacting in small groups during workshops can improve our ability to listen to others and encourage collaboration.

Summary of Skills Gained by Studying Sociology

1) General cognitive abilities and skills:

- judging and evaluating evidence

- appreciating the complexity and diversity of social situations

- assessing the merits of competing theories and explanations

- gathering, retrieving and synthesising information

- making reasoned arguments

- interpreting evidence and texts

- developing the ability to reflect on the accumulation of knowledge.

2) Discipline-specific abilities and skills:

- the ability to formulate and investigate sociologically informed questions

- competence in using major theoretical perspectives and concepts in sociology, and their application to social life

- the capacity to analyse, assess and communicate empirical sociological information

- the ability to identify a range of different research strategies and methods and to comment on their relative advantages and disadvantages

- the ability to conduct sociological research in a preliminary way

- the ability to undertake and present scholarly work

- the ability to understand the ethical implications of sociological enquiry

- the ability to recognise the relevance of sociological knowledge to social, public and civic policy

3) Transferable skills:

- learning and study skills

- written and oral communication skills in a variety of contexts and modes

- statistical and other quantitative techniques

- information retrieval skills in relation to primary and secondary sources of information

- communication and information technology skills

- skills of time planning and management

- group work skills

Source: *QAA Benchmark Statement – Sociology (QAA 2000)*

POST-DEGREE POSSIBILITIES

As Giddens states: 'A sociologist is someone who is able to break free from the immediacy of personal circumstances and put things in a wider context' (2001: 2). Sociologists are well equipped to understand and explain social problems, thereby being in a position to point to possible solutions. Hence, sociology can be practically applied to a range of employment opportunities even though few jobs have a sociology degree as a requirement. A good source of information on the kinds of employment for sociology graduates can be found on the following website: http://www.prospects.ac.uk. Their research found that for sociology graduates in 2001:

68.6% went into employment, which is significantly higher than all social sciences graduates (at 55.3%) and slightly higher than all UK graduates (67.7%). As a sociology graduate the range of careers and potential employers open to you is very diverse and in 2001 has included retail management, public relations, banking, welfare advice, research, accountancy and systems analysis. Typical employers include local and central government, industry, commerce, National Health Service, a wide range of Civil Service departments and agencies, education authorities, further and higher education institutions, media, IT, charitable, counselling and voluntary organisations. (Gray 2003)

So, after your degree you will have a wide variety of possibilities to consider. Given that you may have had the opportunity to learn how to work with large data sets you could consider using these skills by gaining ICT (Information and Communication Technology) related employment. Alternatively you may work for the civil service or local government, for the police or prison service, or in human resources (previously known as 'personnel') or management positions. You may go on to do a law or accountancy conversion. Hopefully your enjoyment of sociology might encourage you to continue studying at Masters or Ph.D. level. Whatever you finally decide, two things are for sure: first, by studying sociology you will develop a greater understanding of social interaction and the social world – surely something that on its own justifies the effort? Second, studying sociology can enhance your academic and communication abilities, your basic organisational skills and help to make you, we believe, a more critically aware and reflexive individual.

FURTHER READING

British Sociological Association (2004), *Giving Sociology a Voice,* updated July 2004. <http://www.britsoc.co.uk> Useful information on what sociology is and what sociologists do.

Cottrell, S. (1999), *The Study Skills Handbook*, Basingstoke: Macmillan. Extremely useful resource for encouraging students to be reflexive about their own learning style and finding ways to improve a range of study skills.

Gray, K. (2003), 'Sociology: Main Areas of Employment', *Graduate Prospects,* University of Edinburgh, updated January 2003. <http://www.prospects.ac.uk/cms/ShowPage/Home_page/Options_with_your_subject/Your_degree_in_sociology/Main_areas_of_employment/p!epjejl>

PART II
Understanding Sociology

3 SOCIOLOGICAL IMAGINATIONS

Getting students to think sociologically is clearly the key objective of any degree in sociology. In this chapter we outline what we think are some of the key characteristics of a recognisably sociological 'way of seeing' (Berger and Kellner 1981) and a 'sociological imagination'. This oft-used phrase was given to us by the celebrated North American sociologist Charles Wright Mills (1916–62) and was the title of his most famous book (1959). In that text he describes the sociological imagination as enabling us to 'grasp history and biography and the relations between the two within society' (Wright Mills 1959: 6). The relation between history and biography, the individual and society, is often seen to be the hallmark of thinking sociologically. Wright Mills goes on to say that:

> No social study that does not come back to the problems of biography, of history and of their intersections within a society has completed its intellectual journey. (Wright Mills 1959: 6)

Wright Mills was a great admirer of the classical sociologists and considered that the sociological imagination, as concerned with the above, was the 'mark of the classic social analyst' (1959: 6). Thus, before saying more about a sociological perspective(s), we shall take a brief look at some key figures from sociology's 'classical period' who continue to leave their imprint on the discipline.

THE EMERGENCE OF SOCIOLOGY

It was once a prevalent belief that sociology was a trendy
subject (somewhat hard to believe now!) and that it was very
much a child of the 1960s. Although this was undoubtedly a
time of great expansion for sociology in many countries in
terms of student numbers, university departments and sociological literature, sociology as a recognised academic discipline has actually been around since the end of the nineteenth
century. Indeed, ideas that could be considered sociological
have been around even longer and pre-date, by hundreds of
years, the formation of a discipline called Sociology. However
it was not until the eighteenth century, in some western
societies, that the social world and society came to be seen
as an object of scientific inquiry and investigation. Scottish
Enlightenment figures such as David Hume (1711–76), Adam
Smith (1723–90) and Adam Ferguson (1723–1816), as well as
thinkers such as Montesquieu (1689–1755), increasingly began to hold up 'society' as a focus for inquiry. Other figures
from this period worth a name-check include Henri de Saint-
Simon (1760–1825), an influential thinker who became the
first and one of the most important analysts of industrial
society. Auguste Comte (1798–1857) was important for developing the first comprehensive system of sociology and for
being the person who gave us the term 'Sociology'.

Thus, the intellectual and critical roots of sociology grew
out of the period of scientific and philosophical development
known as 'the Enlightenment', the intellectual imprint of
which can be found to this day (Ray 1999). The Enlightenment of the late seventeenth and the eighteenth centuries
involved a series of radical shifts in western philosophy and
science. Prominent Enlightenment figures included intellectual
luminaries such as René Descartes (1596–1650), Jean Jacques
Rousseau (1712–78) and Immanuel Kant (1724–1804). 'Reason' and 'Progress' were the rallying calls of the Enlightenment. There was also a general belief that the successes of the
natural sciences could be achieved in the social realm and
harnessed to cut through non-scientific dogma (often repre-

sented by religion and the authority of the monarch) and guide social and human progress through the rational application of scientific principles.

We do not want to reduce the historical trajectory and development of sociology solely to the influence of a few brilliant individuals and their ideas – this would be a very unsociological approach to adopt! Many of those mentioned above developed their ideas within the context of great social, economic and political changes that affected certain areas of western Europe. What emerged out of these changes were the basic structures and relations of a recognisably modern society and this proved to be a catalyst for the development of sociology as individuals tried to understand more fully the world that was emerging around them (McIntosh 1997).

The French revolution in 1789 and the industrial revolution, which began in Britain in the eighteenth century and spread unevenly across Europe, helped usher in the modern world. The French revolution was important for establishing new conceptions of politics and notions of individual rights and questioned the legitimacy of traditional forms of power and authority such as the church and the monarchy. For Kumar, 'No other event in the history of modern times has so powerfully aroused the sentiments of novelty, transformation, and the creation of a new order' (1978: 19).

The industrial revolution heralded a new era of immense productive power and potential, the decline of a rural way of life, the growth of cities and masses of wage labourers, among its many transformations. In essence the incredible power of industrial capitalism was unleashed on parts of the world and its inhabitants, and the central features of modernity were formed – a term we will expand upon in Chapter 6. Many of those at the time who grappled to understand these social changes eventually came to be known as the 'classical sociologists' – even if those individuals may not have thought of themselves as sociologists (Giddens 1971; Hughes et al. 1995; McIntosh 1997). Thus thinkers such as Karl Marx (1818–83), Ferdinand Tonnies (1855–1936), Émile Durkheim (1858–1917), Max Weber (1864–1920), Georg Simmel (1858–

1918), Herbert Spencer (1820–1903) and others, all helped to map out the central concerns and key areas of investigation that would be the preserve and preoccupation of generations of sociologists to come. The following questions became key for sociology's development: what is new about the world; how is modern society experienced; how can some form of order be maintained; how is society possible and how is it maintained; how can we understand the role of the individual within society and the relation between the individual and the social?

The concerns of contemporary sociology have splintered into a bewildering array of new issues and topics. However, many of the questions put on the sociological agenda during the classical period still resonate today, as do the various attempts that were made in order to provide an answer to them. To this extent the sociological imagination still owes much to its classical predecessors. Given this we should out-line, albeit very briefly, what some of the major figures from this time had to say about the modern world they saw around them and give a flavour of their differing sociological imaginations. Specifically we will deal with the work of Marx, Durkheim, Weber and Simmel.

KARL MARX

For Marx, the first human act was that of 'production': production in the broadest sense of activity that humans indulge in to sustain and reproduce themselves. The manner in which they organise themselves, their interaction with the real, material world, was a matter for empirical investigation and Marx utilised the concept of a 'mode of production' as his basic unit of historical categorisation. Thus the capitalist mode of production was a social and historical formation that represented only one particular way to organise economic and social relations. This approach to studying the nature and development of human society became known as 'historical materialism'.

In the *Communist Manifesto* (1848) Marx writes of the awesome productive power of capitalism and of how the 'bourgeoisie, during its rule of scarcely one hundred years, has created more massive and more colossal productive forces than have all preceding generations together' (Marx and Engels 1968: 40), as it has 'pitilessly torn asunder the motley feudal ties that bound man to his "natural superiors" (Marx and Engels 1968: 38; see also Berman 1983). Despite this sneaking admiration for the power of capitalism, Marx was of course one of its fiercest critics and, as a revolutionary, spent much of his life trying to help overthrow it (Callinicos 1983).

Capitalism for Marx was a dynamic, yet inherently exploitative, socio-economic system prone to cycles of booms and slumps. Wage-labour is central to capitalism and being economically compelled to sell one's labour for a wage is the fate of the bulk of the population, given that most people need to sell their labour power in order to at least maintain an 'adequate' standard of living. Marx argues that paid labour within capitalism, a key source of identity as well as money for most of us, can be degrading and 'alienating' as it detaches the worker, in a number of ways, from the process and products of production (Marx 1975).

Marx argued that capitalism was also fundamentally a class-based society. Although well aware that society had many divisions, Marx (and Marxists) focused on two main classes within the capitalist mode of production: the working class (or proletariat) and the capitalist class (or ruling class or bourgeoisie). Class location depended primarily on one's relation to the means of production: essentially, whether you only had your labour power to sell or were in a position to hire labour power and set it to work to create a profit. The antagonistic and exploitative relation between these two classes, in large part, defined the nature and experience of the capitalist mode of production.

Although relatively few people would accept such a bald depiction of capitalism today, it still informs many people's view of the modern world and modernity (see Chapter 6). Similarly, although variants of Marxism (such as Marxism-

Leninism in the former Soviet Union) do not exert the huge influence they once did for much of the twentieth century, Marxist politics and political groups are still a powerful force around the globe today.

Importantly for sociology, Marx(ism) inspired forms of research into the world that are politically engaged. Much feminist scholarship, for example, has taken to heart Marx's famous dictum that 'The Philosophers have only interpreted the world, in various ways, the point, however, is to change it' (Marx 1968: 31) and linked their social research into a 'standpoint' that aims to improve the position of women in society (Smith 1990 see Chapter 4). A similar influence can be found in the sociology of crime and deviance, and the sociology of development (Peet 1991). Marx's detailed analyses and discussions of the labour process within capitalism has influenced generations of scholars in the area of work and employment (Thompson 1989).

ÉMILE DURKHEIM

Durkheim posed some enduring and key sociological questions about how, given the increasing complexity of modern societies, it was still possible for society to 'hold together' and for individuals not to be embroiled in an anarchic free-for-all. It is of course still worth thinking about this question today – how is society maintained as a stable and working (generally!) entity? For Durkheim the solution lay in the kinds of solidarity and morality that bonded individuals together and formed a recognisable and, for him at any rate, a scientifically observable social world. As part of this, Durkheim made a distinction between the 'mechanical solidarity' of traditional societies and the 'organic solidarity' of modern societies. The former emphasises a togetherness based on similarity, whilst the later is a solidarity based on the interdependencies required to maintain a complex society in a state of equilibrium. A perfectly functioning and balanced organic society, however, was something of an ideal, particularly as 'anomie' was an all too common feature of modern societies. Anomie is a key and influential Durkheimian concept and can be understood as a state of 'normlessness' in which individuals become detached from the society they are part of. This can occur due to imbalances in forces of regulation and integration within society. One dramatic consequence of this which Durkheim famously analyses is the change to the suicide rate (Durkheim 1970). An example of this anomic state could be a society in the midst of an economic depression *or* boom in which many individuals become uprooted from friends, family, jobs and other relations and ties that help anchor them into society and to each other – we often hear stories about the lottery winner who becomes ultra-wealthy but lives in relative social isolation. Durkheim was enough of an Enlightenment figure to believe that sociology could be used as a diagnostic tool to improve society and alleviate conditions of anomie.

In *The Rules of Sociological Method* (1982 [1895]) Durkheim outlined his view of how sociology should be conducted. All sciences, for Durkheim, require their own specific object of inquiry and, for sociology, this was the realm of 'social facts'. Durkheim offers two definitions of a social fact: 'every way of acting, fixed or not, capable of exercising on the individual an external constraint' and 'every way of acting which is general throughout a given society, while at the same time existing in its own right independent of its individual manifestations' (quoted in McIntosh 1997: 208). An example of a social fact could be rules of etiquette and manners which we generally follow within a particular society; fashion could be seen as another social fact. These are 'facts' within society that we could resist but it would often be very difficult to do so. Anyone who has endured the social embarrassment of picking up the 'wrong' piece of cutlery at a formalised meal or forgetting to switch off their mobile phone in lectures will realise this! So social facts are not reducible to individuals yet exert an influence on individual behaviour. Such social facts then could be studied and compared between different societies. The key rule for Durkheim was to study social facts as 'things'; that is, we should approach social facts in the same way that a natural scientist, such as a biologist or physicist, approaches their object of study.

Durkheim's insights into crime and deviance – controversially suggesting that a certain level of crime is 'normal' – had a powerful impact on 'labelling theory' in the 1960s and 1970s and on the sociology of crime more generally (see Chapter 8). He continues to influence sociology, most notably in relation to the sociology of religion and functionalist perspectives (see Chapter 4). Of course, as generations of sociology students know, Durkheim is often one of the first sociologists that they encounter in their degrees, and in books such as this!

MAX WEBER

Weber believed that many of the tendencies and institutional arrangements within modern society involved grave consequences for the lives of individuals. Life in modern western societies was, for Weber, becoming increasingly 'rationalised' and the role of the free-thinking individual was increasingly being squeezed out and given less room to flourish. Rationality was the key characteristic of modernity for Weber and pervaded all aspects of social life. This was probably most evident in the bureaucratic forms of organisation that are a commonplace and crucial part of the modern world. For Weber, rationality, or too much of it, can have irrational consequences. Values such as liberty and fraternity and human characteristics such as passion, anger and other emotions can be lost in the drive for efficiency and calculability, particularly within the capitalist marketplace. In his analyses of modern western rational capitalism, Weber thus despaired at what he saw as the increasing domination of instrumental rational (*zweckrational* in the German) action in all spheres of life. This is an approach to life that suffocated and stifled individual freedom and creative expression and led to an increasingly 'disenchanted' world. A superb discussion and comparison of Marx and Weber's accounts of *Capitalism and Modernity* is Derek Sayer's book (1991) of that title.

For Weber western industrial societies were increasingly prone to this 'disenchantment' and ultimately we were perhaps doomed to inhabit an 'iron cage' of rationality – a metaphor that has become one of the most often used within sociology.

Weber's programme for sociology gave a privileged starting point, not to the realm of the social as with Durkheim, but to individual social action. Weber broke down social action into four 'ideal types': instrumental rational action; value rational action; traditional action; and affectual action. The first refers to action that is seen to be the best and technically most efficient way in which to achieve a clearly defined goal – running a business in order to maximise profit is a good example of this form of action. Value rational action relates action to an absolute religious, ethical or aesthetic end. Traditional action is habitual action done primarily because it was 'always done that way' and, lastly, affectual action is action that is determined by the emotional state of the actor, for example anger, elation or depression. Weber suggested that we could use such ideal types to explore 'real' action and behaviour in the social world. Importantly he insisted that an empathetic understanding (*Verstehen*) of human action is possible and could be built into our programmes for sociological research (see Chapter 4).

GEORG SIMMEL

Georg Simmel (1858–1918) was a multi-faceted thinker whose interests ranged across a number of academic disciplines and areas of interest. Befitting a man that was brought up in a Berlin household perched on a busy crossroads, his analysis of the modern 'metropolis and mental life' (Frisby and Featherstone 1997) has been enduring within sociology, as has his extensive studies of money (Simmel 1990). He was also a major influence on the development of symbolic interactionism in the USA. More recently Simmel has become increasingly important as a theorist and analyst of (post)modernity and of culture more generally (Frisby 1992).

In contrast with Durkheim, Simmel rejected any kind of large-scale constructions of society as an object of study for sociology (Frisby and Sayer 1986). Simmel's focus, in terms of his sociological studies at least, was upon forms of 'sociation', however trivial or mundane these might appear. The social world (and sociation) was best understood as interconnected webs of continual reciprocal interaction between individuals. Such sociation was in many ways society being 'done'; society in process. Such an approach was, in part, an answer to Simmel's own question of 'how was society possible?' A Simmelian sociology should therefore investigate, 'the forces, forms and developments of sociation, of the cooperation, association and co-existence of individuals' (quoted in Frisby and Sayer 1986: 57).

This led Simmel to see sociation in the merest fragment of interaction and exchanges and all could be a legitimate source of study for the sociologist. This is the case given that Simmel stressed the 'interconnectedness' of everything, thus in this sense, nothing is to be seen as trivial as everything is related in some sense (Turner 1999). So the busy surface of social life and even the most fleeting of social interactions, a brief conversation or a nod of recognition between two passing strangers in the street contained, in essence, all that society is. It is the amalgam of these interactions that constitute this thing called society and no event or action should have any logical priority over any other. As Simmel puts it: 'Society is not an absolute entity . . . it is only the synthesis or the general term of the totality of these interactions' (quoted in Turner 1999: 149).

Simmel has left us a sociological treasure trove of intriguing essays on such diverse subjects such as the 'stranger', 'secrets', 'space', 'fashion', 'the adventure' and even one on the 'alpine journey' (for more examples see Frisby and Featherstone 1997). Simmel's impressionistic approach and his emphasis on modes of experiencing the flux of the modern urban world, as well as the subject matter of his studies, have made him an important figure in the sociology of culture. Coupled with a rising interest in post-modernity (see Chapter 6), Simmel has been drawn back into the sociological spotlight after a long time on the sidelines of the classical canon.

Hopefully we can see, even from the above glimpses at the sociological imaginations (Wright Mills 1959) of the classical theorists, that they have each provided a powerful and rich legacy from which we can draw on when thinking about the key interests of sociology. Obviously a great deal more could be said about these approaches and no doubt will be during your degree. Meanwhile to expand your understanding of these scholars you could look at Ray (1999) and Turner (1999).

ON THINKING SOCIOLOGICALLY

The above discussion of the emergence of sociology, and brief look at the perspectives of some of its 'founders', should have already given you a flavour of what thinking sociologically may entail. Further, as we have seen from the above, sociology is not some kind of closed system with clearly set rules and procedures. What sociology is, and what sociologists do, is open to interpretation and it is all the more interesting and lively for it. However, most sociologists develop a sense of judging whether something is 'sociological' or not and if a piece of work is starting to stray off into the realm of other disciplines, typically history, economics or psychology. Given this, it would be useful for us to be a bit more specific about what we think undergraduate students should understand by way of a sociological approach to the world.

As part of discussing what thinking sociologically entails, Bauman (1990) emphasises the use of 'responsible speech'. Bauman is not being moralistic here, rather he is making the point that we need to be systematic and measured in our use of speech, words and concepts. We can perhaps draw a distinction here, as many sociologists are wont to do, between a 'sociological sense' and a 'common sense'. Common sense is of course very difficult to define, for example the question 'common to whom?' immediately springs to mind. However, it is useful to invoke this somewhat mythical beast in an attempt to emphasise what a 'sociological sense' is.

In our everyday discussions and conversations about various issues and topics we are not normally expected to be consistent every time we use a particular word or phrase, to provide evidence for most comments we make or to define every term we use. This would make light-hearted banter in many social situations extremely difficult, if not impossible – it would also make much of our social interaction extremely tedious and boring. You may want to attempt conducting yourself in this manner in a range of social contexts (at home, in a café, having a drink with friends and so on) and see how long it takes for the interaction to break down and for tempers to flair! (Such so-called 'breaching' experiments were made famous by the sociologist Harold Garfinkel (see Chapter 4), the founder of ethnomethodology.) However, within the academic context of essays, reading and workshops, aspiring to such forms of consistency is entirely appropriate and will not be frowned upon. So, for example, when you use terms such as 'society', 'crime', 'deviance' and 'patriarchy' in an essay you should do so in such a way that you try to make clear your understanding of such notions. You should also attempt to be consistent in their usage.

In the world of common sense there is also little requirement to be 'scientific'. Relatively few sociologists would argue that their subject area is a 'hard science' such as physics, and more than a few would argue fervently against any such notion. However, almost all sociologists would not deny that adopting some of the standards and benchmarks of a 'scientific' approach should be part of how we conduct sociology. This is a point that we elaborate on in relation to our discussion of positivism so we will not repeat ourselves here. Suffice to say that, some dissenters aside, there would be general agreement that some form of evidence should be provided – either (or both) of a qualitative and/or quantitative nature (see Chapter 5) – to substantiate what is being asserted.

We should construct logical arguments, make clear our theoretical standpoint and outline our research methods (i.e. the manner in which we may have gathered any data; see Chapter 5). We would normally attempt to relate what we have learned to a wider social context and make some broader, more general, claims on the basis of our more specific research. For example, we should bear in mind that we rarely have the time, inclination or resources to interview everyone connected with our area of interest!

Bauman (1990) also suggests that we should strive to 'defamiliarise the familiar' when thinking sociologically. One way to develop this skill and mindset is to act and think like a 'tourist' within your own environment. By this we do not mean that that you should stop and ask people directions in the street and walk around clutching a guidebook! Rather, tourists are often good intuitive sociologists as they often seem to find everyday things interesting, even those we may have become so accustomed to we barely notice them. So, suddenly the design on a banknote, the manner in which people greet each other, the way people order food in cafés, how people queue for a bus, can all appear strange and worthy of attention. It is well worth trying to adopt the inquiring gaze of the tourist in our own societies. This can have the effect of giving us insight into how the world came to be the way it is, how it is maintained and perhaps alert us to the fact that it can be organised in a variety of different ways. Therefore, an appreciation of movement and change as well as understanding continuities is crucial, we would argue, to developing our sociological imaginations (see Chapter 6). This alerts us to the socially constructed nature of the social world, a facet of sociological thinking that we should discuss further.

SOCIAL CONSTRUCTION

Social construction, or social constructionism, and its proper application is contested within sociology. Nevertheless, some version of this concept is generally accepted to be an important part of a sociological imagination and as a 'way of seeing' sociologically (Berger and Kellner 1981). At times such an approach is associated with particular authors (most notably Berger and Luckmann 1967) and sociologies informed by the philosophical tradition known as phenomenology (discussed in Chapter 4). However, it is often used in a more general manner to emphasise the way in which sociologists understand how the social world is constituted and maintained. This is the sense in which sociologists might suggest that something is socially constructed. Many years ago Simmel was right to warn against the overuse of this term and the attempt to try and explain everything as being a social construction as this can lead to a kind of sociological determinism in which crucial biological and natural aspects of the world and ourselves are downplayed. After all, having brown eyes is hardly best explained as being a social construction (mind you, what constitutes the colour 'brown' is!). However, grasping the socially constructed nature of our world, and the myriad ways we behave within it, is a central component of being able to think sociologically.

Generally, sociologists are not impressed with arguments that revolve around the position that certain aspects of the social world, and people's behaviour, are seen to be 'natural' or 'just the way things are'. For example, you may have often heard just such arguments in relation to the natural differences between the behaviour of men and women. Sociologists would argue that many of these supposed differences and 'normal' behaviours are not natural but are socially constructed. 'Gender' is the word sociologists use to emphasise that very few of the behaviours, mannerisms and actions of men and women can be explained due to biological and anatomical differences. Thus, people act out and internalise, to a greater or lesser extent, roles, norms, attributes and mannerisms that are deemed to be 'appropriate' for men and women to display and to adhere to. This happens through powerful, and often subtle, processes of 'socialisation'. We can be socialised into behaving like a man or woman 'should' or 'ought' to. In this sense we are socialised into our genders from the beginning of our lives, and it is a process which never stops. For example, as babies, boys tend to be dressed in blue and girls in pink. Not only are they given different clothes and toys, but they often play different games such as boys play with guns and girls with dolls. There is nothing natural about these distinctions as these are social conventions that can vary across societies and over time.

Processes of socialisation are never total nor complete. There is always room for individuals to resist and exert their agency (see below). We only need to look around the world at different cultures and at the same societies at different time periods to appreciate the huge variety of behaviours that men and women display. Think of the notion of the tom-boy or cross-dressing for example – perhaps you can think of others yourself?

We can think of many things in our society where it can be useful to invoke notions of social construction and socialisation. Examples could include the behaviour and dress of people from different age groups and forms of manners and etiquette. It can also be useful to understand apparently scientific forms of measurement as being socially constructed. For example, statistics used to measure and represent such things as the rate of crime and unemployment can be usefully understood as social constructions, a point we will explore more fully in Chapter 8.

HISTORICAL SPECIFICITY

Karl Marx, particularly in his scathing criticisms of political economy (Marx 1954), had a powerful sense of the need to place events and things in a historical context. Although it may appear that parts of the social world are fixed and given in our lifetimes, over the course of a generation or two social change(s) can be rapid to the point of being overwhelming. Think of the sudden demise of the former Soviet Union in 1989. Less dramatically, how many of us, say ten years ago, would have predicted the widespread use of the mobile phone in the UK? It is also worth reflecting on the new and evolving forms of etiquette that are still being established with their use

– for example, is it acceptable or rude to use a 'mobile' when we are out for a meal? Basically, things change over time.

Although much about the social world can give the impression that it has 'always been that way', we should be aware that it changes, at times dramatically and at other times incrementally. Given this, we need to build into our theories, methods and our 'sociological imaginations' an ability to appreciate and incorporate movement. We should appreciate the 'historically specific' nature of many social forms and configurations.

AGENCY AND STRUCTURE

As we suggested at the beginning of this chapter, probably the most distinctively sociological characteristic of thinking sociologically is the focus on the interaction and relation between the social and the individual, or to use the more technical terms, agency and structure. The ways in which a person relates to the social context or group, how we understand the position and influence of the individual social actor and the way his or her actions and intentions are enabled or constrained by society and the power of collective groupings, has been a constant feature of the sociological imagination. It would be difficult to improve on the following description of the issue as posed by Philip Abrams, which is worth quoting in some length:

> How do we, as active subjects make a world of objects which then, as it were, become subjects making us their objects? It is the problem of individual and society, consciousness and being, action and structure; a problem to which the voices of everyday life speak as loudly as scholars. It is easily and endlessly reformulated but, it seems, stupefyingly difficult to resolve. People make their own history – but only under definite circumstances and conditions: we act through a world of rules which our action creates, breaks and renews – we are creatures of rules, the rules are our creations: we make our own world

– the world confronts us as an implacable and autono-
mous system of social facts . . . The estranged symbiosis
of action and structure is both a commonplace of everyday life and the unbudgeable fulcrum of social analysis.
(Abrams 1982: xiii–xiv)

The dichotomy between agency and structure causes some
controversy in sociology as to how useful a distinction it really
is. Much of this is unnecessary if we take a sensible approach
to it. It is simply a model to understand the world and it is the
interaction between agency and structure, how it works out in
practice, that should be borne in mind – all polarised dichotomies only exist in people's heads after all!

Nevertheless, the tension between agency and structure can
be a useful starting point for thinking sociologically about the
world. For example, consider fashion for a moment. When
you go into a shop to purchase a particular piece of clothing,
what forces are at work in the moment of buying? Are you
making a decision based solely on your own choice? Or are
you buying particular items because you want to be like others
you see as being significant? More likely it is a combination of
the two 'forces' which are implicated in the outcome, but what
is the balance involved and how can we explain this (see
Albrow 1999; Berger 1970; Jenkins 2002)? When understood
this way, and applied to the world around us, the concepts of
agency and structure can be a great aid to developing our
sociological imaginations.

FURTHER READING

Bauman, Z. (1990), *Thinking Sociologically*, Oxford: Blackwell. This is an excellent
    and thought-provoking introductory text. The second edition (2001, co-authored
    with May) is also recommended.
McIntosh, I. (1997), *Classical Sociological Theory: A Reader*, Edinburgh: Edinburgh
    University Press. This text provides a good selection from the writings of Marx,
    Weber and Durkheim.
Wright Mills, C. (1959), *The Sociological Imagination*, Harmondsworth: Penguin. A
    sociological classic and still worth consulting.

4 THEORISING THE SOCIAL WORLD

Sociological theory often has the effect of sending students running for cover and cowering with trepidation. Such theory anxiety is a common occurrence among sociology undergraduates, and for many of those who have long since completed their degrees! There is no point in denying that a lot of theory can indeed be difficult and challenging. Given the complexity of the social world and the apparently endless opportunities it offers for divergent interpretations and perspectives, we should not be too surprised that the theories that have developed to understand the world around us can themselves be complicated and abstract. However, theory and theorising is intended primarily to help us better understand the social world, and some of the best theories are characterised by their simplicity and elegance rather than their obscurity and complexity.

It is also worth bearing in mind that we are *all* capable of theorising and this is something we do all the time (Best 2003). The social world which we are a part of is not self-explanatory. It is full of events, things and interactions that we do not always fully understand and find difficult to explain. Our relationships with other people, for example, can often be hard to fathom and we continually have to make decisions about how best to proceed at any one point. This is the case with many aspects of our life from the relatively trivial, such as supporting a football team, to the more serious, such as getting a job or dealing with illness. Many of the gaps in our knowledge about such things have to be filled by us on the basis of assumption, guesswork, past experience and predicting what we may think will happen in the future. In trying to make sense of the often complicated world in which we live we do this routinely; indeed it would be difficult to go about our daily business if we did not. You may want to reflect upon the strategies you adopt to deal with any uncertainties and ambiguities you encounter as you conduct your everyday routines.

This is the kind of mental work that human beings carry out all the time and in essence this is a form of theorising. Human beings are perhaps above all 'thinking' animals, even if this may not appear to be the case at times! Thus theorising, philosophising and being reflexive are not activities that are alien to us but something that we do at times almost spontaneously and at other times with much more deliberation, either way it is part of what makes us human.

Some people spend a large amount of time philosophising and theorising about the social world and often write this down for others to read. Some of them even get paid to do this! Clearly in the long history of people thinking and theorising systematically about the world and rewriting, debating, arguing then retheorising again and again, a great deal of written theory has been generated. This continues as you read this and will do so long after you stop. So basically there is a lot of theory out there, some of which is encased in large and imposing 'theory books'. This is the more formalised form of 'theory' that students encounter when they embark on their degrees. Sociology students will have to grapple with a significant amount of this kind of theory during their studies.

So, what is theory? Given what we have said above you should probably be able to have a good stab at answering this question – perhaps before you read any further you should try doing just this. Essentially a theory is a set of propositions that try to explain phenomena and events in the world. Consider the following statements: 'unemployment can be caused by falling wages' or 'crime is more likely to occur in societies that are unequal'. Both these statements represent forms of theorising in that they are making connections between relatively discrete events and predicting some likely outcomes. Neither may prove to be true but at least they can guide our research and the methods we choose to verify or falsify such statements. So theories in sociology try to shed light on particular aspects of the social world. Sometimes they do this by focusing upon a small, perhaps minute, part of the social world, such as micro-interaction in a small group. Approaches in this tradition would include symbolic interactionism and ethnomethodology (see below). Other theories may tackle much bigger concerns, for example, the development of the global economy. This more macro-approach could be the preserve of functionalism or variants of Marxism. However, no matter the scope or concerns of the theory, all try to do the same sorts of things in terms of helping us approach and formulate the question(s) we want to ask and answer, focus on what we should study and make sense of the data we gather.

Within sociology many of the theories we use are not of the concise and precise nature adopted by 'hard' sciences such as physics or even other social sciences, namely economics or psychology. Sociological research seldom employs theories of the 'if A and B occur then C' or 'x + y = z' variety and rarely is there an expectation that it should. This is not to say that we should not strive towards the precise formulation of research hypotheses (more often the somewhat less precise phrase 'research questions' is employed) or attain consistency and rigour in our sociological theorising and research. Nevertheless it does have the 'honesty', born of necessity perhaps, of acknowledging the complex and shifting nature of the social world that we study and that always striving to find precise answers to questions is probably a forlorn, if not pointless, task. It is also perhaps an overrated objective given the history of 'precise' answers that turned out to be wrong! It is worth noting however that this reflects *our* understanding of the general tenor of contemporary UK sociology; within the US for example there is a much greater emphasis on more quantitative and 'scientific' approaches to sociology. So even sociology is historically and culturally specific; we should be sociological about sociology.

In our experience, many sociologists who carry out interesting and excellent research would often be hard pushed to give a precise theoretical label to what they are doing and would *not* be able to easily answer the question, 'What theory are you using'? Thus we have to be wary of the somewhat artificial, formalised and neatly packaged presentation of theories and theorists we find in the literature and the much more messy and nuanced way in which theory is drawn upon and utilised by practising sociologists. Not being able to 'name your theory' does not of course mean that what you are doing is without theory or not theoretical, for reasons we have just elaborated. Research and writing can still be theoretically informed and recognisably sociological due to the way they are conducted, the questions asked and the incorporation of elements of a sociological imagination as outlined above in Chapter 3.

Similarly, as will become apparent in Chapter 5 most sociological work does not involve a clear-cut distinction between theory and research methods, that is the ways in which we conduct our research and gather data. There is a much more messy and symbiotic mix between theory and methods in sociological work. One informs and interacts with the other and it is often impossible to tell where one finishes and the other starts. This should be seen as part of the same research *process*.

So, theories in sociology are often grouped into perspectives or schools often for the convenience of teachers of sociology and writers of textbooks (see Best 2003). Again we have to be wary of overemphasising differences as boundaries are often not so blurred. That said, however, let us stick with established convention and run through the main theoretical perspectives in, and influences upon, sociology.

POSITIVISM

French philosopher Auguste Comte (1798–1857) is generally regarded as the founder of positivism – his 'positive philosophy'. The versions of positivism that have become important for the social sciences generally, and sociology in particular, emphasise the centrality of an empiricist approach. Empiricism rejects as pointless concerns with 'essences' and the 'nature' of things, rather we should only deal with phenomena that we can systematically observe, measure and involve in repeatable experiments. Positivists (not that many people would give themselves this label!) would argue that the social sciences such as sociology should endeavour to replicate and adopt the approach and methods (not to mention the success and status) of the natural sciences such as biology and physics and apply such scientific approaches to our study of the social world. The inner-states of humans, the meanings they attach to their actions and the experiences they have cannot be directly observed and studied 'scientifically' and thus should be dismissed and left for unscientific speculation and meta-physical musings.

Very few sociologists would accept this strong positivist position and there are numerous criticisms of positivism. You may want to think about the problems associated with study-ing the social world in such an empiricist manner and consider how much would be left out of your positivistic gaze. For instance, what of the meanings individuals attach to what they do? Indeed, it is this whole world of human meaning and subjectivity which many sociologists have argued marks it off completely from the natural world – think of all the 'unob-servables' out there such as love, hate and fear and the contents of our minds? As a consequence the methods of the natural sciences, some would argue, are completely in-appropriate for the study of the social world (for a discussion see May and Williams 1998).

However, notions of science and rigorous research are still an overriding concern for many sociologists and given this, positivistic approaches leave their mark on much of what sociologists do. Questions of validity and reliability, appro-priate methods of data-gathering and well-defined research questions continue to be central issues to those who carry out sociological research (see Chapter 5 for a fuller discussion of these issues). In this way the basic tenets and principles of positivism continue to exert a significant and pervasive influ-ence on the way sociology is conducted.

PHENOMENOLOGY AND HERMENEUTICS

It is worth drawing your attention to two other modes of philosophical activity and inquiry – phenomenology and hermeneutics (Moran 2000). No sociologists that we know of would describe themselves as 'phenomenologists' or 'hermeneuticians' (were such a word to exist), but both of these philosophical endeavours have left a lasting legacy on how sociology is understood and conducted.

Phenomenology is essentially a form of philosophical method that was developed primarily by the German philosopher Edmund Husserl (1859–1938). Within sociology it is most often associated with Alfred Schutz (1899–1959). Husserl wished to get back to 'things in themselves', that is to arrive at the essential features of any given thing or object. In order to do this we have to rid ourselves of what we already know and try to retrace the way that our consciousness comes to know 'things in the world'. We can do this, according to Husserl, by a process of phenomenological reduction, or epoche, until we reveal the true 'essence' of things.

Schutz, a one-time pupil of Husserl, developed a more sociologically orientated phenomenology which gives primacy to 'lived experience' in the everyday lifeworld (the German word commonly used is *Lebenswelt*). Schutz sought to explore the way people experience this lifeworld and the 'natural attitude' (a term borrowed from Husserl) adopted by individuals in order to make sense of it. For Schutz, the manner in which people form meaningful interactions in this 'intersubjective' world (namely, the fact that we live among other thinking individuals) was of interest. Thus a phenomenological sociology would place an emphasis on the way individuals go about their daily lives and how they manage to make order out of the potentially infinite flow of information that they receive. For example, when you meet a friend for coffee in a café, you would make sense of this interaction on the basis of 'stocks of knowledge' that you have built up in previous encounters.

Hermeneutics shares many of the concerns of phenomenology but is generally more narrowly understood as the science of interpretation. The term was derived from the work of medieval monks who interpreted sacred religious texts in search of their 'true' meaning. Hermeneutics really came to the fore, and took on its more modern usage, during the long-running dispute between German academics in the late nineteenth century over the approach and methods to be utilised in the human sciences (Anderson et al. 1986). Essentially, this was a debate about whether the approaches of the natural sciences could be utilised when studying human history and society.

In the social sciences a hermeneutic approach places an emphasis on meaning and human action (Bauman 1978; Giddens 1976). Hermeneutics also emphasises understanding the relation of the part to the whole, of appreciating the context within which an action takes place and relating that part back to the whole again – a procedure known as the 'hermeneutic circle'. For example Max Weber, who was embroiled in the aforementioned debate, urged sociologists to incorporate an empathetic understanding and interpretation (or in German, the well-used term *verstehen*) of human action in their studies of the social world. Perhaps, for example, by trying to empathise with the meanings and motives of football supporters, or individuals who take part in extreme sports, we can make much more 'sense' of their actions than we could through merely observing their actions.

These approaches rarely emerge in an undiluted form within sociology but, rather, have had major impact on various sociological approaches such as symbolic interactionism and ethnomethodology. As such they ask different questions and utilise different methods (see Chapter 5) from more positivistic and quantitative approaches. Sociologies influenced by these traditions focus on meaning, interpretation and the way the world is socially constructed and understood intersubjectively. Classic examples of such a phenomenologically informed sociology can be found in Berger and Luckmann's *The Social Construction of Reality* (1967) and Garfinkel's *Studies in Ethnomethodology* (1967). (For a phenomenologically informed investigation into young people's understandings of welfare, see McIntosh 2003.)

FUNCTIONALISM

This was a dominant paradigm in sociology – particularly in the United States – after the Second World War. Functionalism attempts to understand the role different parts of a society have in maintaining a society as a whole. The different functions and roles of various rules, customs and traditions are thus assessed in terms of their 'function' to society, how they relate to each other and keep a particular society in some kind of 'healthy' state or balance. Functionalism tends to draw upon biological metaphors and language. Society is often compared to or understood as an organism with 'needs' and 'wants' and could be in a state of decay or in 'good' or 'bad' health with conditions that were considered to be pathological for its well-being. One of the great classical sociologists, Émile Durkheim, is often associated with this form of thinking and utilised such metaphors – but to categorise such a subtle and wide-ranging thinker as a functionalist is to do his legacy a severe injustice. The influential anthropologists A. R. Radcliffe-Brown (1881–1955) and Bronislaw Malinowski (1884–1942) also famously utilised a functionalist approach in their studies of 'primitive' societies. In more recent times North American sociologists Talcott Parsons (1902–79) and R. K. Merton (1910–2003) developed functionalist approaches that came to dominate North American sociology for decades; it never had the same prominence within Europe.

To give an illustration of a functionalist approach it may be useful to draw upon Merton's famous distinction between 'latent' and 'manifest' functions. This distinguishes between the purpose individuals may ascribe to a particular activity and the function that it can serve for the wider collective or society. For example, a functionalist anthropologist may be told by members of a 'primitive' society that the purpose of performing a rain dance is to end a drought (its manifest function). However, the somewhat sceptical anthropologist may surmise that whilst such dances do not affect the weather, they can have an important role in maintaining group solidarity and identity (its latent function). People may have all sorts of reasons and motivations for getting married or maintaining a monogamous relationship whereas, taking a broader view, the functionalist may argue that social arrangements such as marriage and monogamy are beneficial for the smooth functioning of the society at large.

Parsons built on his readings of Durkheim and Weber, and in *The Structure of Social Action* (Parsons 1937) he outlined his influential 'action frame of reference' with which he could analyse social action. Action for Parsons involved five constituent elements: the 'actors' themselves; the 'goals' they intend to achieve; the 'means' they use to achieve them; the 'norms' by which people conduct themselves; and the 'conditions', or context, within which people act. By means of this approach Parsons, and others, tried to investigate the relation between the structure of the 'social system' and the actions of individuals. As part of this, processes of socialisation were considered important. This refers to the way in which we learn and absorb from an early age, the norms, roles and rules of particular social formations. This allows for some kind of broad 'consensus' that maintains social systems in a state of 'order' and stability.

A regular criticism of the functionalist approach is that it has an inherent tendency towards conservatism. Thus, present social arrangements are often seen to be best for 'normal' social functioning. So, because things have been organised in a particular way for a long time there can be an assumption that that is the way it should stay in order to maintain a properly functioning society. Such an emphasis on continuity and stability leaves functionalism open to criticisms that it cannot account for social change nor conflict within society. The overuse of the organic metaphor, comparing human society to a biological organism, is also a source of criticism. The assumption that everything in society serves some kind of function to the maintenance of that society can lead to an overly simplified understanding of a complex and contingent social world.

However, functionalism and its off-shoots such as consensus theory and structural-functionalism still exert a pervasive (some may say pernicious) influence within sociology. More recent theorists, who prefer the term neo-functionalist or systems theorists (for example, Niklas Luhmann), have done much to revive the functionalist tradition. Functionalist metaphors and terms continue to be part of the vocabulary of sociology, indeed it often seems difficult for many students (and lecturers) *not* to compare society to a living organism in their written work.

THE INTERACTIONIST TRADITION

Approaches such as functionalism tend to take a large-scale macro-perspective. Other approaches in sociology focus much more closely on smaller forms of micro-interaction. One of the most important and enduring sociological perspectives in this vein is that of symbolic interactionism. This emanated primarily from North America, although the European classical tradition was a major influence. It has its roots in the North American philosophical tradition of pragmatism, of which G. H. Mead (1863–1931) was a key figure. Mead is generally acknowledged as the central influence in the development of symbolic interactionism, although the history of the term and its development is far from being clear cut or easy to trace (see Plummer 1996).

The title of Mead's posthumously published book (1934) gives a clue to his interests: *Mind, Self and Society*. Mead emphasised the importance of language and symbols within human communication and the way in which understandings of the 'self' and 'others' are formed and re-formed in the experience of our interactions. Such insights were drawn upon and developed in a number of ways within symbolic interactionism. While the symbolic interaction perspective is sometimes associated with Mead, it was Herbert Blumer (1900–87) who took Mead's ideas and developed them into a more systematic sociological approach and who coined the term symbolic interactionism. Interactionist sociologies place a focus on the everyday micro-world of human communication, in many ways the very stuff of the social world that we inhabit. Emphasis is placed on the way people exchange and understand meanings within social interaction. The social world for the interactionist is a fluid and dynamic place, constantly being made and remade and in a state of 'becoming'. It is thus the emergent properties of social life that the interactionist explores.

It may seem that in much of our routine interactions nothing of any significance takes place. However, a huge amount of information, visual and non-visual, can be exchanged in a short time between individuals. Subtle changes in body movements and facial expressions can radically change the meaning of our communication as can the context within which it takes place. For example, think about the way in which our tone of voice, the raising of our eyebrows, or dismissive hand waving can alter the meaning of our interactions. Also the social and physical context of our interaction can alter our communication. So depending on whether we are in a church, a football stadium or at a university seminar will have a big bearing on how we understand our and others 'appropriate' behaviour. To add to the complexity, much interaction and communication changes over time and across cultures. For example, think of rules of etiquette and notions of appropriate dress during the Victorian era compared to now. In relation to cultural differences, shaking your head from side to side in India indicates a yes. All in all it is quite a lot for us to take in! We can see why Harold Garfinkel (see below) suggested that conducting social life is something of a 'skilled accomplishment'. Of course we become aware of the complexity of social life when it all goes horribly wrong, when we loose our 'social skills'. Saying the wrong thing at the wrong time or incorrectly picking up what people say can make us feel extremely uncomfortable and all too acutely aware of the fragility of social life.

Erving Goffman (1922–82) was one of the most influential sociologists of this micro-world of human interaction. Although categorising the idiosyncratic Goffman as a symbolic interactionist is somewhat problematic, he is often closely associated with this tradition. In a number of celebrated studies such as *The Presentation of Self in Everyday Life, Asylums, Where the Action Is, Encounters* and *Stigma*, Goffman brilliantly analysed and dissected the minutia of human interaction. In his early work Goffman developed his notion of 'dramaturgy' and the 'dramaturgical' metaphor. Essentially this involved comparing social life to a stage or theatre within which people engaged in 'impression management' and played out a number of roles. Goffman also discusses the ways in which we can adopt and discard particular roles within certain contexts via his notions of 'back stage' and 'front stage' performance. A good example of this would be the way in which a waitress conducts herself in front of customers compared to her behaviour in the kitchen away from clients. Further explorations by Goffman on the ways in which people with 'spoiled identities' are 'stigmatised' (see Goffman 1963) and on the characteristics of 'total institutions' such as prisons and hospitals have also had a lasting influence (see Goffman 1961).

ETHNOMETHODOLOGY

Ethnomethodology is the most phenomenological of all recognisable traditions in sociology. Harold Garfinkel (born 1917) is generally regarded as the founder of this approach and his *Studies in Ethnomethodology* (1967) is its foundational text. Ethnomethodology shares many of the methodological and investigative approaches of symbolic interactionism. In many ways it is a much more radical approach and, according to ethnomethodologists at least, exists on the periphery of, and in an uneasy tension with, conventional or mainstream sociologies (Cuff et al. 1992). Indeed, although it seems hard to credit now, ethnomethodology was the catalyst for many an angry exchange between sociologists, some of whom thought ethnomethodology was undermining, from within, conventional sociological approaches.

Garfinkel was heavily influenced by the phenomenological sociology of Schutz and Parsons' structural functionalism, at least in his reaction and critique of Parsons. Ethnomethodology tackles the problem of 'voluntarism', a criticism often levelled at macro-theories such as functionalism. This refers to the long-standing problem of the relation between agency and structure (see Chapter 3). Within big theoretical systems, such as functionalism, individuals can often appear to be 'cultural dopes', that is, they are at the mercy of society and powerful social forces. Instead of seeing people as some kind of puppets controlled by the strings of socialisation, Garfinkel wanted to stress the manner in which they actively and purposively engaged in, and created, the world around them.

We can get by in our social world by making assumptions that others share a common taken-for-granted knowledge about the world, even though this knowledge is partial and incomplete. This world of commonsense knowledge and practical reasoning is the subject matter and object of inquiry of ethnomethodology: how do people actually *do* things in the world? For ethnomethodologists how people 'do' being a mother, lawyer or policeman can be studied empirically. Consider the fact that you will soon be a student. What does 'be a student' actually mean? How will you relate to other students, what kinds of things will you talk about, how will you know how to conduct yourself in lectures and workshops, what are the common stocks of knowledge that you will routinely draw upon when being a student? Studies of talk and conversation analysis (something of a sub-discipline within ethnomethodology) are key concerns to ethnomethodologists in their analyses of locally produced knowledge. From his own website Garfinkel posits the main concerns of ethnomethodology:

A selected corpus of ethnomethodological studies offers evidence for locally produced, naturally accountable phenomena of order, logic, reason, meaning, method, objective knowledge, evidence, detail, structure, etc., in and as of the unavoidable and irremediable haecceity* of . . . ordinary society. (Garfinkel 2004) [* best understood as referring to the 'here-and-now']

So ethnomethodology seeks to understand the practical methods whereby people, in their interaction with others, make the social world intelligible. Hence, we derive the term 'ethno[-people]-method-ology[the study of]' (Sharrock 1986).

The complexity and subtlety of the ideas involved in ethnomethodology cannot be dealt with here but two key concepts are worth further consideration: indexicality and reflexivity. Indexicality refers to the way that words, language and concepts develop meaning only within the context of their use, so meaning is never fixed, given or clearly known to us. However, we can 'gloss' over these gaps in our knowledge and still continue to act meaningfully. For example, transcripts of telephone conversations often appear to be full of meaningless random words and sentences and non-words ('ummm', 'uha' – listen for some others) but at the time they are uttered they can make, if not perfect, certainly 'good enough' sense. Reflexivity refers to the ways in which people (ethnomethodologists often use the term 'members') when describing, referring to or naming things or events are also giving sense to them. So rather then mere description they are, in practical ways, *creating* these activities and events. So when you and your friends are discussing a party from the night before you are actually making sense of the actions and behaviour of the various people who were there. You are not just mechanically describing what took place but are providing context, meaning and actively creating and re-creating events and the characters involved – assuming you can remember what took place of course!

In a series of 'breaching' experiments Garfinkel demonstrated the fragility of this knowledge. He asked his students to constantly ask the question 'What do you mean?' in their interaction with others – you can try this and watch how quickly your smooth social interaction descends into chaos!

STRUCTURALISM

Terms such as 'structuralism', 'structuralist' and other variants crop up a lot in sociology and can refer to any approaches, such as functionalism and variants of Marxism, which give priority to social systems and structures over individual agency and social action. More often, however, it is a term which applies, albeit loosely, to a method of inquiry that has influenced a wide range of academic disciplines.

Structuralism derives from linguistics: the study of the form and function of language. Ferdinand de Saussure (1857–1913) is regarded as the modern founder of linguistics and structuralism can reasonably be seen as an attempt to 'apply his linguistic theory to objects and activities other than language itself' (Outhwaite and Bottomore 1994: 737). Saussure saw language as a total system within which words and speech utterances get their meaning through their difference from other words – for example an apple, as we know, is not a pear or a banana and the meaning of the word apple is understood in relation to its difference from these other types of fruit (and fruit is understood in relation to vegetable, and so forth). So Saussure was interested in the 'deep structures' that underpin our use and understanding of language – the hidden rules of the game that allow us to make sense of the bewildering variety and complexity of language and speech that we are confronted with. In this way structuralists try to get behind the continually changing surface of social life to tap into the reality that lies beneath. As Anderson et al. suggest, structuralism emphasises that the 'diversity of surface appearances masks the unity of structural realities' (1986: 102). Structuralism is holistic in approach in that it considers the relation of the part – be it a particular action or event – to the whole.

The structuralist approach differs from most conventional

sociologies as it, somewhat controversially, leaves almost no room for concerns with history and the human subject - 'the spoilt brat of history' as Lévi-Strauss provocatively put it. So, rather than incorporate the passage of time (a diachronic approach) and human agency, structuralism is characterised by a snapshot (or synchronic) approach which, of course, emphasises structures. The concern is with more or less constant forms and structures over ever-changing content. This has left it open to accusations that people are reduced to mere puppets of the system (Thompson 1978).

Claude Lévi-Strauss (1908–) applied such an approach in his influential anthropological studies and sought to uncover in the innate workings of the mind universal categories of thought which were common across all types of cultures and societies. The stamp of structuralism and post-structuralism can be found in a wide range of subjects and is associated with key (mostly French) figures such as psychoanalysis (Jacques Lacan and Julia Kristeva); literary criticism (Jacques Derrida); semiology (Roland Barthes) and Marxist philosophy (Louis Althusser) (for a discussion see Belsey 2002).

In terms of sociology the most influential structuralist thinker, and probably the only one you will have to tackle head on in your sociology degrees, is Michel Foucault (1926–84). Foucault's interests ranged far and wide but there are central themes in his work, his discussion of which has proved to be influential within sociology. Foucault is concerned with the manner in which human subjects have been created ('subjected') through the workings of power and processes of classification. The growth of the state and state power and the increasing need to regulate, classify, administer and pacify growing populations resulted in a 'carceral society' of workhouses, prisons and asylums. As part of this, technologies of power and discipline have became pervasive throughout modern societies (Foucault 1992). For Foucault it makes more sense to talk of the way in which individuals are 'subjected' rather than active historical subjects. For example, constructions of sexuality for Foucault are a consequence of just such concerns with classification, whether it be heterosexuality or homosexuality, which can have the effect of limiting our freedoms of expression and making us conform to, and internalise, appropriate forms and norms of behaviour. Foucault's insights have impacted on the analysis of governance, the workings of power and have provided key insights for post-modern and feminist theory.

FEMINISM

Feminism (or to be more accurate 'feminism*s*') exerts a significant influence throughout sociology. Whilst not all sociological research can be described as 'feminist', most research has to consider issues that feminists have largely put on the agenda. So, in our experience at least, most sociologists would be unlikely to generalise grandly about the world on the basis of research that just included male respondents or interviewees – unless the research was *specifically* about men of course. Some degree of gender awareness is now the norm within most sociology (it would be somewhat utopian of us to write 'all'). Most obviously, articles sent to academic journals will be rejected out of hand if they use an overtly masculinist language, for example, constantly using 'him' or 'his' when you may not be referring to only men, and terms such as *man*kind and *man*power. This is a point to be borne in mind when you are writing and submitting undergraduate essays.

Feminist ideas (and, of course, the depressingly stubborn resistance to them) have been around for a long time. The classic early statements can be found in Mary Wollstonecraft's *A Vindication of the Rights of Women* (1792) and John Stuart Mill's *The Subjection of Women* (1869). These texts, and others, addressed the inequalities women face in relation to men. In more recent times, various strands of feminism have emerged from Marxist feminism, through liberal feminism to radical feminism (for a comprehensive review see Tong 1989). A shared concern amongst all these feminisms is, of course, improving the position of women in relation to men.

'Patriarchy' is the term used to describe a wide-ranging set of social relationships that favour men and maintain male privilege (Walby 1990). Such male power can be seen in most spheres of contemporary society – consider the world of paid employment and politics for example (see Chapter 7 for evidence of this). It is worth saying at the outset that the power men have over women is not total or complete and is often contested, resisted and successfully subverted. You will no doubt be aware of powerful and successful women in many areas of social life. Your own experiences will also provide you with examples of the ways in which the inequalities between men and women are not clear cut and can be barely visible within numerous interactions and relations. Women are clearly not a homogenous group and feminist scholarship now acknowledges the varied life experiences of different groups of women in terms of race, class and sexuality (Jackson and Scott 1996).

However, men continue to hold on to much power and privilege in a society like the UK, not least through the threat of, or actual, male violence towards women. Away from the 'public sphere' and in the 'private sphere' women are responsible for the bulk of childcare, and housework still falls predominantly to women, something which feminist scholars brought into public debate (Oakley 1974). Not that there is anything inherently inferior in such tasks as doing the washing-up or hoovering a carpet as compared to building a brick wall or doing the company accounts. Yet the former tasks, under *present* social arrangements, are generally seen to be of lower status than the former. It is these unequal relations of power between men and women that unites all feminisms together and is the focus of feminisms' theoretical and empirical endeavours.

Many of the inequalities between men and women are often 'explained' (dismissed may be a better word) in relation to essential differences between men and women, such as women are somehow more suited to doing housework than men. Feminist writers have led the way in disputing such essentialist arguments and make a distinction between 'gender' and 'sex'. Sex is thus a biological category based on anatomical differences whereas gender refers to a process of socialisation that defines 'masculinity' and 'femininity'. Expectations follow about appropriate, suitable forms of masculine and feminine behaviour and the kinds of things men and women should or should not do. Such ideas are, of course, historically specific and not fixed or given. Thus feminist writers point to the socially constructed nature of such categories and emphasise the ways in which they can be challenged, changed and subverted (Smith 1988).

FURTHER THEORISING

In this chapter we have introduced some of the more prominent and influential forms of theorising within sociology. The confines of space have made this a rather selective discussion and there are other theoretical positions and approaches we could have introduced you to. These include actor network theory, queer theory, critical theory and also the work of important authors such as Anthony Giddens (Craib 1992a) and Pierre Bourdieu (Jenkins 1992). But such delights will have to wait until later in your studies!

Hopefully, in this chapter we have given you a good indication of the scope and diversity of what makes up sociological theorising. The way in which we use and borrow from theory depends on our interests and the question we ask. We do not have to devote ourselves solely to one particular theory over another and we emphasised at the beginning of this chapter the interconnectedness of much sociological theory. However, a good knowledge of the kinds of theoretical work that has been done under the umbrella of sociology is indispensable for properly understanding the subject at degree level.

FURTHER READING

Best, S. (2003), *A Beginner's Guide to Social Theory*, London: Sage. This is a comprehensive and lively introduction to social theory, even if it tries to be a bit too provocative at times.

Craib, I. (1992b), *Modern Social Theory: From Parsons to Habermas*, 2nd edn, London: Harvester Wheatsheaf. A wide-ranging and reader-friendly text.

May, T. and Williams, M. (eds) (1998), *Knowing the Social World*, Buckingham: Open University Press. This book contains good discussions of the issues involved in theorising and researching the social world.

Outhwaite, W. and Bottomore, T. (eds) (1994), *The Blackwell Dictionary of Twentieth-Century Social Thought*, Oxford: Blackwell. An indispensable guide to a huge range of theories, theorists and concepts from sociology and beyond. A superb source book that would prove useful throughout your degree. Some of the entries could have been written more clearly however.

5 RESEARCHING THE SOCIAL WORLD

Compared with a theoretical and abstract subject such as philosophy, sociology is a much more empirically orientated discipline. What do we mean by this? Well, by saying this we are drawing a close connection between what sociologists do and the 'observable' world 'out there'. There is a generalised concern within sociology to link and substantiate theoretical positions and statements with some form of data and evidence. Important consequences follow from this, not least that a wide range of techniques and skills have developed within sociology in order to collect the types of evidence and data that we want. This is what is being referred to when people talk about 'methods' within sociology.

Relatively few people who would describe themselves as sociologists would also regard themselves purely as theorists and a quick glance at any sociology journal would confirm the reliance on some form of evidence to substantiate any claims that are being made. Sociology can be more or less theoretical or empirical, but very little sociology (that we know of) can be described as being completely one or the other. Indeed, we would go as far to say that it is actually impossible to be absolutely empirical or absolutely theoretical. All 'facts' in a sense are theory laden and theories normally arise as a consequence of reflection or puzzlement over some part of the world out there (see Chapter 3). Albrow puts it well when he says that 'No research can work without theory, even when it denies it has any. For theory simply means the connection of ideas. Even counting is theory' (Albrow 1999: 41).

However, sometimes making distinctions between theory and method can be useful; as an analytical separation it is probably unavoidable. When planning a piece of research it can be practical to dichotomise between the two activities – if only to fit on a form somewhere! As undergraduates, writing a dissertation for example, you may well be asked questions about your theoretical approach and the methods you plan to utilise. However, given what we have said above, you should realise by now that in practice the distinction is something of a false one. Given this, it is probably best to talk of a research *process*: a process where emerging data, theories and methods are in a constantly shifting balance and relation.

Let us try to illustrate this with a brief example. We may be interested in the way young people use their leisure time. If so, we would immediately start to think about issues such as the age group we were interested in contacting, the kinds of leisure activities we have in mind and what we mean by the term 'leisure'. It could be that we narrow down our area of interest to looking at young people's choice of nightclubs during the course of five weekends in a large town in the north of England and we want to ask as many young people as possible about this. Questions of method will soon confront us, such as, *how* will we conduct such a study. We may arrive at a possible figure of 200 young people to seek opinions from. Interviewing this many people can be done but it would be time consuming and expensive. So perhaps distributing and collecting questionnaires at the nightclubs in question would be an alternative method to adopt. They could be posted out, but then we would need to get addresses from somewhere and perhaps have to accept that many would not be returned. We could stand outside nightclubs and ask a brief set of questions. This raises issues not only of personal safety, but of travel and access to the nightclubs and of how much time we can devote to speaking to respondents.

Thus, much research in sociology is a combination of what, why and how questions as well as a series of practical considerations over cost, time and access. The way in which we respond to these issues and questions will impact on our decisions about what methods we choose.

QUESTIONS OF EPISTEMOLOGY

As we have seen from Chapter 4 there are different theoretical traditions in sociology and these are associated with different approaches to the gathering of evidence and data. The kinds of methods that you adopt will, in large part, depend on the types of questions you want an answer to and what part of the social world you are exploring. Such issues relate to what is known as *epistemology*. This is a branch of philosophy which explores and raises questions about our knowledge of the world, where this knowledge comes from and how we judge between different kinds of knowledge (Audi 1998). So we engage with epistemological questions whenever we start to form our research questions and plan the ways in which we want to answer them.

The various methods in sociology are generally gathered into two types: *quantitative* and *qualitative*. Broadly speaking a quantitative approach involves large-scale research: collecting and analysing numerical data. A qualitative approach tends to be smaller in scale and is more concerned with seeking out the meanings and understandings associated with social action. Yet again we should be wary of getting too fixated with the differences between these approaches and also recognise that many studies are done utilising both quantitative *and* qualitative methods. However, there are differences, often of emphasis, between quantitative and qualitative approaches – the pros and cons of which are discussed below in relation to some specific methods. Choosing between these approaches will involve you in competing forms of knowledge production and questions of epistemology.

Thus, if you are interested in understanding the meanings individuals attach to certain activities, say being part of a political party, then you may want to spend some time with them at their meetings and observe their behaviour over a period of time. This could be augmented with semi-structured interviews (discussed below) with a relatively small number of selected individuals. In this way you would be generating knowledge that was, to use terms introduced in Chapter 4, more in the tradition of hermeneutics and phenomenology and qualitative in nature. However, getting an overall picture of the voting behaviour of millions of people in the UK would tend to lead you towards the use of large-scale survey methods that involved substantial, or even huge, numbers of respondents. This would allow you to make more valid statements about UK voting trends as a whole. Such an approach would be more quantitative in character.

Let us now look a bit more closely at three of the most commonly used methods in social research: surveys, interviewing and ethnography. Surveys and structured interviewing use a quantitative approach to research, whereas unstructured and semi-structured interviewing and ethnography fall within the qualitative tradition.

SURVEYS

A key, and well-established, quantitative research method is the survey. The British National Census, for example, is based on surveys that have been conducted (every ten years) almost continuously since 1801. Surveys come in a number of forms but they are generally organised in such a way as to gather large amounts of data from big samples. What do we mean by a sample? Essentially a sample is a piece of a much larger whole, or population, a term given to the total numbers of individuals or units that comprise the group to be studied, such as the total numbers of prisoners in the UK. In this case you would include in your sample a certain percentage of the total population of British prisoners.

To give another example of sampling, in order to assess the amount of hours people in the UK spend watching the television it would be impractical, not to say impossible, to contact and interview the millions of individuals who watch television every day. So the next best thing is to gather data from a much smaller, more manageable, sample of individuals who are representative of the total population of television viewers. This needs to be done with some consideration. For instance, to only include the TV habits of 85-year-old men in your sample would limit the general claims you could make regarding the population of TV viewers as a whole. However, a sample that included a large number of respondents and a spread of variables such as age, gender and social class would allow you to make more sensible claims about the total population. If your sample mirrors the population as a whole, your generalised claims would have a degree of 'validity' and representativeness – that is, your results would give you a truer picture of the subject under study (McNeill 1990). Samples come in different shapes and sizes. Some can be randomly produced from a sampling frame. This is the complete (or as complete as possible) list of the total numbers in a particular population – the UK electoral roll is a commonly used sampling frame. Others can be built up from specific quotas of individuals on the basis of such characteristics as ethnicity, gender or age.

Surveys often consist of interviews that run through a highly structured set of themes and questions – you will no doubt have tried to avoid a market researcher clutching a clipboard and pen in the street! Questionnaires are the most common tool used in a survey and are essentially a list of questions that the researcher will ask. They may consist of both closed questions (questions that require a set response like yes or no) and open-ended questions (when respondents articulate their views in their own words). In quantitative research the basic idea behind the questionnaire is that the same questions will be asked in the same way in each interview carried out. This maintains a high degree of 'reliability' and repeatability in the research, which means that it can be conducted in the same way (or as close to the same way as possible) time and time again. Such efforts to maintain reliability in quantitative research is seen to be important in order to compare research conducted at different times, such as the UK Census, and in different places (Dixon et al. 1987; Gilbert 1993)

Postal questionnaires can be sent out to large numbers of individuals as a method on their own or to complement interviews (often in the form of follow-up questionnaires).

However, response rates (that is the percentage of those who actually fill out and return a postal questionnaire or take part in a survey) can be poor. The same problem can emerge from the use of the internet and telephone-based surveys. Face-to-face interviewing can also be problematic for a number of reasons, such as: the skill of the interviewer; the willingness of the interviewee to talk and the fact that people being interviewed can often say what they think the interviewer wants to hear. All of these problems compromise the validity of the methods employed.

However, the large numbers involved in many social surveys and large data sets form the basis by which representative and reliable data can be provided. For example 5,500 households (over 10,200 individuals) form the basis of the *British Household Panel Survey*. You should check the Economic and Social Data Service website at http://www.esds.ac.uk/longitudinal/access/bhps/ for details on how this survey is conducted and the huge array of data it produces (see Bryman 2001 for a discussion of large data sets).

Large volumes of data also allow for sophisticated statistical analysis to be conducted. The techniques involved are outside the scope of this book, but are an important part of sociological knowledge about the world (for a good introduction to quantitative data analysis see Bryman 2001 and Gilbert 1993). Even sociologists who would not describe themselves as being quantitative often rely on 'big' statistics and data for getting a general picture of the area they are looking at, such as rates of unemployment, information on the health of a population or levels of poverty in a society.

INTERVIEWING

It has been suggested that around 90 per cent of research in the social sciences involves some kind of interviewing (Holstein and Gubrium 1997). The accuracy of this estimate is hard to gauge but it is certainly the case that interviewing is a central method within sociology. There are three main types of interviewing: structured, unstructured and semi-structured. Structured interviewing is based on a standardised format with questions that are fixed. This type of interviewing conforms to the above mentioned quantitative approach to research and uses a questionnaire as the research tool. There is no flexibility: each person interviewed should be asked exactly the same questions, in the same order so that the responses can be directly compared. The interviewer has to stick to the set interview and should not probe, or follow up, responses with additional questions. Structured interviews are intended for large-scale research in order to quantify responses to particular questions and subsequently generate statistics with the results to prove or disprove particular hypotheses.

In contrast, qualitative interviewing adopts a more interpretative approach (see Chapter 4), concerned with seeking people's understandings of their social world. Thus, it is usually small scale and in depth as it attempts to tap into the meanings people attach to events and relationships in their lives (May 1997: 130). Burgess refers to qualitative interviews as 'conversations with a purpose' (1984: 102) as the researcher has a reason for conducting them but they are only loosely structured, if at all.

Semi-structured interviews tend to be based around some key themes but have a very flexible format so questions can be asked in a different way or order. Usually an interview guide is used to remind the interviewer of the main issues which should be covered, but the interview may digress or go back and forth between the topics. Thus a flexible style of questioning is employed in order to clarify, expand, probe and follow up the issues as they arise. However, there is some broad structure so that responses can be compared to a certain extent.

Unstructured interviews are even more informal and are non-standardised. Hence, they are extremely open and flexible, although there is usually a particular theme around which the conversation is focused. They include the life-history interview which is based on someone's biography, during which interviewees recall life events and reflect upon the ways in which their beliefs and perspectives have changed over time. Informal interviewing may also be a spontaneous chat about a particular issue, which is recorded in a notebook afterwards. This very informal kind of interviewing usually takes place alongside other methods, for example as one of several techniques used within an ethnographic approach to research (see below).

Interviews are mainly just conducted with one individual at a time but can also be carried out in pairs or small groups with approximately 3–12 people. These are often referred to as the 'focus group' interview where a discussion revolves around a particular topic of interest. The interaction between the members of the group encourages brainstorming and can generate a range of perspectives on the same issues. As with any research method there are both advantages and disadvantages to using either group or individual interviews. The benefits of a group interview is that the dynamics between people in the group can be interesting and they may spark ideas off each other which can enhance the group discussion. Participants may be more relaxed and less intimidated in a group situation, especially if they are being interviewed with people they know. However, some people prefer the privacy of an individual interview which gives them more opportunity to discuss their personal experiences. Furthermore, it may be more difficult to record and analyse what is said during focus groups compared with an individual interview.

Combining both focus groups and individual interviews can also be beneficial. For example, in a research project on teenagers' problems (Punch 2002), group discussions were used to explore the key topics openly and broadly, whilst giving the participants the opportunity to define the important issues to be examined in more depth in follow-up individual interviews. The group situation was perceived as useful for gaining confidence with their friends, building rapport with the interviewer, memory prodding and as a warm-up discussion to the individual interview. The young people could check out and become familiar with the researcher as well as with the research. The focus group produced more socially acceptable 'group' responses about the ways in which young people generally deal with their problems. The individual interviews then enabled the teenagers to raise more personal issues which they may not have wanted their peers to know about. In the one-to-one interviews the young people could share more personal thoughts and experiences not only because it was more confidential but also because it was easier for them to speak freely and in depth without interruptions (see Punch 2002).

Overall, the key strengths of qualitative interviews are that they offer an opportunity to explore the depth and complexity of the social world from the research participants' point of view, thereby tapping into their interpretations and understandings. Thus the interviewees' accounts are the interview 'data'. Consequently, we need to recognise that what people say they do is not always what they do in practice. Sometimes it can be useful to combine interviewing with observation in order to cross-check people's interview accounts with everyday situations, but this is not always feasible.

One of the limitations of using interviews is that we have to rely on people's views as told in the interview situation. We have to bear in mind that 'an interview is a social encounter like any other' (May 1997: 129) so the kind of data we generate will depend on how well the interviewer has managed to build rapport and a relationship of trust with the interviewee. Thus interviewing depends on a high level of interviewer skill, particularly in relation to that person's ability to communicate effectively with people who are possibly from a range of different backgrounds.

ETHNOGRAPHY

The term ethnography is usually associated with observational methods and can be defined as 'the art and science of describing a group or culture' (Fetterman 1989: 11). Hammersley and Atkinson suggest that:

In its most characteristic form it involves the ethnographer participating, overtly or covertly, in people's daily lives for an extended period of time, watching what happens, listening to what is said, asking questions – in fact, collecting whatever data are available to throw light on the issues that are the focus of the research. (1995: 1)

Thus, ethnography is a qualitative approach to research which often includes semi-structured or unstructured interviewing. However, the main method of ethnography is participant observation, which is when researchers directly participate in the lives of the group they are studying for a relatively long period of time. This kind of fieldwork is often referred to as 'being in the field'. By being involved in their everyday lives, the researcher can become closer to an adequate understanding of the group's culture and lifestyle. Ethnographic research tends to consist of close observation of what people are doing as well as conversations ('informal interviews') with them in order to inquire about the meanings they attach to their actions.

There are several different types of participant observation depending on the extent to which researchers become active, or detached, observers in the culture they are studying. These different roles of the researcher are referred to as the complete participant, the participant-as-observer and the complete observer (Gold 1958). The complete-participant role is when the researcher totally participates by becoming a full member of the group. For example, the researcher obtains a job as a waiter in order to observe the other waiters in their world of work. This kind of research is carried out covertly, which means that researchers hide their identity and the people being studied do not know that they are being observed. There can be many ethical dilemmas associated with this kind of covert research and generally it is not widely practised (for a fuller discussion see Bulmer 1982; Homan 1991). However, some researchers argue that it can be the only way to observe particularly powerful groups in society, such as the police (Punch 1986).

With the role of the participant-as-observer, the research is carried out overtly and the group knows it is being studied. The researcher actively participates in the lives of the group whilst observing at the same time. This role enables the researcher to ask questions and keep notes, as his or her identity as researcher is fully known. The researcher as complete observer does not interact with the group but merely remains as a more detached onlooker. For example, some people who do research in schools sit at the back of the classroom to observe what is happening rather than participate directly themselves. In such research, it is hoped that their lack of participation means that the situation they are observing is less likely to be affected by the researcher's presence as he or she is not directly involved in the action.

However, with an ethnographic approach we have to accept that researchers, in any of the above three roles, may influence the research context since they become part of the social world they are studying (Hammersley and Atkinson 1995). Researchers need to reflect constantly on how their presence may be affecting the social processes that they are observing. Hence, most ethnographers keep a regular field diary where they maintain a record of observations of the ways in which the participants respond to their presence and to the research.

The strength of ethnography is that it enables researchers to explore, in depth, the ways in which a particular group experiences its social world. The research is conducted over time, thereby producing rich detailed information that could not be gathered in a one-off interview or questionnaire. Participant observation provides a way to get to know people better and build trust. It is also an ideal opportunity to carry out informal interviews and talk about issues as they occur, turning conversations to certain topics of interest. In addition, by participating in people's everyday lives, the researcher is able to learn 'by doing', which increases the depth of understanding of the group's activities.

However, one of the key limitations of this method is that it can only be carried out with small numbers of people as it takes time to build rapport and a relationship of trust. Thus it is very time-consuming and can also impose on participants' time and privacy. Furthermore, it can be difficult to compare the different sorts of data obtained since each situation is different and not easily comparable. It relies heavily on flexibility, making the most of opportunistic moments in the field and cannot be easily planned. Consequently, the researcher needs to be very flexible and skilled at building relationships. Another potential drawback of participant observation is that researchers become too immersed in the culture they are studying and loses the professional distance required to analyse the emerging data. This is known as 'going native', as researchers' sociological thinking becomes clouded because they are too personally involved and can no longer relate what they are researching to a wider picture.

SOCIOLOGICAL RESEARCH

We have seen from the above that there are a variety of techniques which can be used when conducting social research. Each method has a range of advantages and disadvantages attached to it, so there is no one single magic method. The methods that are chosen depend on the research topic, the questions that are being asked, the skills of the researcher and practicalities, such as the amount of time and money available for conducting the research. Researchers often adopt both quantitative and qualitative approaches to combine the benefits of both of them. Using a mixture of methods is known as 'triangulation', as two or more methods are used to complement each other as well as to cross-check the validity of the findings.

The research process is often a complicated and messy affair during which many ethical and methodological issues have to be tackled. During your degree you will progressively learn more about the dilemmas involved in conducting sociological research (see Robertson and Dearling 2004). You are likely to have an opportunity to carry out some of your own research, and this often forms the basis for a final year dissertation. You will then have to consider fully issues of research design, sampling and negotiating access, research ethics and data analysis. For now it is worth bearing in mind that there are a range of different approaches to studying the social world and that each has its strengths and weaknesses.

FURTHER READING

Gilbert, N. (ed.) (1993), *Researching Social Life*, London: Sage. A wide-ranging introduction to the issues, techniques and methods involved in social research.
Bryman, A. (2001), *Social Research Methods*, Oxford: Oxford University Press. An excellent and comprehensive introduction.

PART III
Themes and Issues in Sociology

6 THE CHANGING SOCIETY?

Understanding, explaining and conceptualising social change has long been a central concern of sociologists. The classical sociologists from the mid-nineteenth century, for example, were all preoccupied, in one way or another, with social change. The social world, whether viewed from a macro- or micro-perspective, is not static but is in a constant state of flux and movement and a continual and emergent state of becoming. Given this, an awareness of change and movement is very much part of a sociological imagination (see Chapter 3). Sociologists will, to some degree, be tuned in to perceiving change in the research they do; it will be on their sociological radar. So a sociologist interested in researching alcohol consumption in the UK, or doing an ethnography of a gym, will *not* approach such topics with concepts, categories and theories which are designed to capture only that which is fixed and static.

This is not to say that there are not important stabilities and continuities in the world and that change may be slow to the point of being imperceptible, in the short term at least. We should avoid overemphasising the changing nature of the phenomenon which we study. As Miles says, 'There may be a case for arguing that social theorists are predisposed or pre-programmed to exaggerate the degree of social change that they are trying to account for' (2001: 164). We should, then, be perceptive to the ways in which social phenomena and arrangements can be resistant to change. So, for example, the inequalities of power and opportunity that can still be found in British society between men and women has been resistant to change for a depressingly long time. In contrast, the collapse of the USSR was notable for its rapidity and unexpectedness. Thus the relations and tensions *between* change and continuity are central to our sociological understanding of the world around us.

Contrasting terms and dichotomies have often been employed in sociology to help conceptualise the relations between continuities and change. Examples of this from the classical canon would be Durkheim's mechanical and organic solidarity (see Chapter 3) and Tonnies' well-used distinction between *Gemeinschaft* and *Gesellschaft* (in English, 'community' and 'society', see Chapter 8). More recently, distinctions between 'industrial society' and 'post-industrial society' and 'modernity' and 'post-modernity' have been employed. It is important to bear in mind at all times that these polarisations are somewhat artificial and are generally intended to be used as models to help us study and explain certain events in, or states of, the world. We should beware of falling into the trap of believing such clear-cut dichotomies actually exist! Contingency, overlap and complexity are more the norm than clearcut divisions. With this caveat in mind, we can look below at some of the ways such terms have been employed and at other issues in sociology which involve understandings of change and continuity.

ON MODERNITY

Modernity is something of a catch-all term that has been much used in sociology in the last two decades or so. Perhaps predictably there is no clear consensus about what it actually is or refers to. Certainly, the notion of modernity is closely associated with the western world and highlights the contrast between modern society and other less modern societies. In this sense it is a western-centric notion. Kumar goes as far to say, with some justification, that 'it is the principle of western society as such' (quoted in Outhwaite and Bottomore 1994: 392).

Most sociologists would demarcate the term from similar looking and closely related terms such as modernisation and modernism, so let us briefly discuss these terms. The former term found wide currency from the late 1950s onwards, particularly in the USA. Underlying the modernisation of many societies (the USA being the exemplar of this) was seen to be the relentless, and overwhelmingly positive, logic of industrialisation. As (some) societies moved away from a dependence on agriculture and a rural way of life and became industrialised, it was argued that they began to share some key characteristics. These included a detailed division of labour (a specialisation of tasks and occupations throughout society), the development of a factory system, the general application of scientific methods to increase productivity and the growth of a mass of wage labourers. Industrial society was also an urbanised society as people moved away from the country to live, work and play in cities. These all represented massive social changes.

There was believed to be a 'convergence' in the development of industrial nations and a presumption of widely shared common economic goals such as increasing productivity, maintaining economic growth and raising the 'standard of living' and material wealth for the bulk of the population (Cohen and Kennedy 2000). The somewhat rosy glow put upon such industrialisation by writers such as Rostow (1983) and Kerr (1983) is clearly not without some foundation. During the 1960s the increase in economic growth and productivity, and the rise in purchasing power of the average person-in-the-street was a major social transformation. Many people were able to buy into a 'way of life' that only a generation or so earlier would have seemed unimaginable. Holidays in other countries, air travel, fridges, televisions, cars and all manner of goodies came within the financial reach of vast numbers of individuals; essentially the 'consumer society' was born. This generalised affluence and purchasing power also allowed for such developments as the growth of a 'teenage' market whereby 'teenagers' became a distinct and separate consumption grouping with their own fashions, music and lifestyle – a forerunner of more contemporary youth subcultures.

Over time, using levels of material wealth as an index of

individual well-being and wide-scale social improvement came to be seriously questioned. Ecological disasters, such as huge oil spillages, acid rain and global warming (to name but a few), have seriously undermined the positive attachments to the relentless drive to increase productivity and our 'standard of living', making many question exactly what 'progress' is (Lipietz 1989). Perhaps there are other, less materialistic and eco-friendly, ways to live? In addition workers' unrest and/or student protests across many industrialised nations and growing social inequalities across a wide range of indicators within, and between, nations further undermined the positive connotations of modernisation.

The term modernism is used to describe and define sweeping changes in the world of art, architecture and literature at the end of the nineteenth century. Artistic movements such as, for example, surrealism, impressionism and cubism are associated with the modernist movement. Wider social changes (some of which have just been mentioned above) and innovations in science (for example Einstein's theory of relativity) can be included in wider interpretations of the term. Indeed, the awful destructive power and potency of modern warfare may also be seen as emblematic of modernism and the modern world.

But what of modernity? Well, essentially it refers to the state or quality of being 'modern', of being part of, and experiencing, the modern world in which we live. Consider the differences between coming from a country such as the UK and one such as Afghanistan. Modernity encompasses the above-mentioned features such as the dynamism and consequences of capitalist industrialisation, an urban lifestyle and a reverence for, or at least implicit faith in, science and technology. In addition, nation-states (for example 'Britain' or 'Italy') are central to modernity and provide the social and political context within which people live and also are a key source of individual and collective identity (so, people can consider themselves to be 'British' or 'Italian' for example). Identity will be discussed more fully below.

The belief that 'change' is a constant part of our experience and condition is central to the experience of modernity and modern life. You may have heard some people bemoan the fact that 'things never stay the same' or some other such expression. The constant need to change and reinvent the present, the 'tradition of the new', is a phenomenon that only relatively few generations have experienced and only in certain parts of the globe. Fragmentation, transience and a sense of bewilderment and loss accompany the rush to produce and reproduce ever anew. Marx's oft-quoted phrase from the *Communist Manifesto* (1848) puts it superbly when he wrote that 'All that is solid melts into air' (Marx and Engels 1968: 38). The non-stop pressures of competition within capitalism meant that change, movement and the production of new commodities became a built-in feature of capitalist modernity and marked it off from the much more static and essentially rural world of feudalism. Weber, another influential classical analyst of modernity, was dismayed at the inexorable spread of rationality in all spheres of social relations (see Chapter 3). This was epitomised by growing role of bureaucrats and the bureaucratic organisation in modern life.

The negative features of modernity have long been recognised as part of its condition. As early as 1835 the French politician and sociologist Alexis de Tocqueville (1805–59) travelled, as did many other writers and intellectuals, to observe a rapidly expanding Manchester, the first truly industrial city and regarded as a great symbol of the modern age. Tocqueville captured the two sides of modernity when he wrote, 'From this filthy sewer pure gold flows. Here humanity attains its most complete development and its most brutish; here civilisation makes its miracles, and civilised man is turned back almost into a savage' (quoted in McIntosh 1997: 4). To give an even more extreme example, Bauman (1989) analyses the ways in which the methods and awesome power of industrial, scientific and bureaucratic techniques were used to terrible effect during the Holocaust, resulting in the mass production of death.

The main features of modernity then are those associated with 'developed' industrial-capitalist societies – essentially, western society (Said 1978). There has been, and still is, much discussion within sociology as to the validity and accuracy of the term modernity and as to whether we have moved into a new or later phase such as post-modernity (Hall et al. 1992).

POST-MODERNITY

For many sociologists, and others, modernity has come to an end and it is more appropriate to now speak of *post*-modernity. Post-modernity refers to a huge range of social transformations and conditions which include changes to art, culture, film, literature, politics as well as group and individual identities. Key writers such as Lyotard and Baudrillard have argued that we have moved into an era beyond modernity. The world that we inhabit in the early twenty-first century no longer in essence resembles the world gazed upon by the classical sociologists of the late nineteenth and early twentieth centuries. Perhaps, the question runs, we have entered a new social and cultural epoch and we need to rethink the way we understand the world and our relationship to it and each other.

Although one of the features of modernity was its dynamism and changing nature there were, it is argued, key stabilities and continuities. These formed something of a framework around which people could organise their lives to some extent. Being a 'citizen' within the context of a particular nation-state with an accompanying national identity was important for understanding your 'self' in relation to others. Regular employment was also a source of stable relationships and an identity for many (particularly men), for example, as a miner, accountant or train driver. Commitments to economic growth and a reliance and belief (not complete or uncritical of course) in science and technology also marked out the contours of modernity. The organisations and institutions of some form of welfare-state provision were also important in providing a more stable backdrop to people's lives. So, modernity was dynamic but still maintained some key certainties.

Post-modernity, in contrast, offers no such stabilities and we now have to face up to contingency, ambivalence and uncertainty (Bauman 1991). Lyotard (1984) (in)famously stated that the post-modern condition is characterised by an 'incredulity towards meta-narratives'. He was referring here to macro-theoretical understandings of social development, for example, Marxism and functionalism (see Chapters 3 and 4). Notions of progress and reason, guided by grand understandings of the social world and historical development, make less sense within the more fractured world of post-modernity. Post-modernists instead prefer smaller-scale and more localised understandings of the social. Plurality and heterogeneity are central features of the post-modern condition and we need a sociology that can accommodate this and we should enthusiastically embrace and celebrate 'difference' (Urry 2000).

Media such as film, TV, mass-circulation newspapers and the 'web' bombard us with a never-ending stream of images, stories and versions of the 'truth'. Coping with (or embracing, depending on your viewpoint) this world of shifting multiple realities is a key characteristic of the post-modern milieu and *Zeitgeist* (the spirit-of-the-times). Can we actually know what reality *is* anymore? Post-modernity has a certain depthlessness, and trying to call upon science to establish the truth is seen to be an outmoded pursuit. Think of the nonsense often passed off as 'news' in the tabloids. The influential post-modern writer Baudrillard even posed the deliberately provocative question as to whether the first Iraq war (we could also add the second?) actually happened, or was it merely one more media event. Clearly this was not the case but in terms of the ways in which many of us experience such occurrences – we can also think of famine and other 'disasters' – then comparing it to other media events, entertainment even, does not seem too erroneous.

Within post-modernity signs, images and words have become detached from their anchors and no longer have a clear reference – meaning becomes problematic and is up for grabs. Brand names, designer labels, digital technology (can we really say that the camera does not lie anymore? – if we ever could!), cinema and literature all make up a world that it is 'hyper-real', one which is fleeting, ephemeral and discontinuous.

Marx suggested that 'All science would be superfluous if the form of appearance of things and their essence directly coincided' (Marx 1981: 956). However, the surface of the post-modern world is now where we are 'at' – there are no essences just appearances. As a result science loses its modernist role of getting beyond appearances. Consequently, the post-modern world cannot be properly understood via the same perspectives and theories that we have used to understood modernity. Following Lyotard (1984) one could argue that post-modernity inherently involves flux, change and fragmentation thus the big, all-encompassing, theoretical perspectives (such as functionalism and structuralism) have become outmoded and increasingly irrelevant.

POST-INDUSTRIAL SOCIETY

Some of these discussions echo slightly earlier debates about 'post-industrial' society (Bell 1974), a term that continues to be influential within and beyond sociology. The move into post-industrialism is generally seen to be a positive social change and was a consequence of the decline of the manufacturing sector and the growth of new kinds of occupations in the 'service' sector (Hall et al. 1992). The jobs in finance, insurance, health, education and the arts, for example, would be seen to be typical of the kinds of occupations people have in post-industrial societies. Such a scenario is often portrayed positively as it was seen to signal the end of the drudgery and grind of the kind typified by manual factory work. Computers and information technology would allow many of us to concentrate on more creative pursuits involving the manipulation and processing of knowledge. Many criticisms of post-industrialism can be made that we do not have the space to rehearse here (see Marsh et al. 2000). However, it is worth bearing in mind that many of the changes that inspired talk of post-industrialism often appear within debates about post-modernity.

IDENTITIES

Social changes, as outlined above, can involve changes to our identities. How do we understand ourselves in relation to others and how do we understand and react to our interpretation of how others view and understand us? If that all sounds a bit complicated we apologise, but then social life often is! It is not only individuals we have to think about but also their relation to groups and collectives and even whole societies. In this respect you may want to ask a number of questions such as: do I feel part of a larger collective? How important is this and how is it maintained? How do we know we are part of a larger group and how do you decide who is 'in' or 'out'? These are the kinds of questions that sociologists ask when thinking about identities. G. H. Mead (1863–1931) famously made a distinction between the 'I' and the 'me'. The 'I' is the hidden inner self and the 'me' is the outer self which forms as a consequence of interaction with others in the social world. The point being that much of our understanding of who we are is born out of, and formed within, our social interaction with others: we make assumptions about how others see us and react accordingly and so on and so on . . . To put it more simply, I am what I think you think I am!

Identities also imply who we are *not*, so the notion of the 'other' is crucial in this respect (Jenkins 1996). The other can embody who we are different from as well as similarities we may have. Think, for example, of identities that revolve around being 'gay' or 'straight', 'black' or 'white', 'man' or 'woman'. National identities are often maintained through contrasts with those we are not. One example is the way 'Scottishness' and being 'Scottish' is sometimes defined in contrast to notions of 'Englishness' and being 'English' (McIntosh et al. 2004). You should try and think of other examples.

Within modernity, as described above, class, nation and our employment are some of the classic sites of identity which are now seen to be eroding and of less relevance within a postmodern context. So, for example, due to the effects of globalisation (discussed below) people may be less inclined to identify with a nation-state and a specific national identity, thus becoming, for example, less British or French and more European. It has also been argued that the role of employment has become less central to our identities (Beck 1992; Offe 1985). As a consequence, post-modernists argue that identities today are less permanent and more fleeting and fluid than in the past. Thus, we may be involved in a particular lifestyle for a certain time, see ourselves as a parent at another, be part of a short-lived political campaign, a leisure pursuit, an artistic endeavour, a big sporting event or a whole range of different activities. The involvement within each activity will be accompanied by a sense of who we are in relation to those we are doing it with at the time. The point is that these can change and we may have multiple senses of who we are and thus our identities can be fluid. We may even be able to choose among a range of differing identities on offer. Similarly, notions of sexuality such as gay, straight, trans- or bisexual can be played with and dominant discourses of heterosexuality can be resisted, subverted and boundaries blurred. So the post-modern world is one of heterogeneity and a celebration of difference and diversity rather than the more homogenised identities that existed in (some people's version of) modernity. For some, this post-modern world can be seen as liberating and can provide numerous spaces to develop, indulge and play with different conceptions of the self and form multiple individual and collective identities (Hall and du Gay 1996).

'POST', 'LATE' OR 'RISK'?

Some critics would argue that much of the post-modern vision and associated theories make an awful lot of not very much (Callinicos 1989). Others argue that the demarcation between modernity and post-modernity is a rather forced and artificial one and there is an over elaboration and exaggeration of tendencies and characteristics which were already present within modernity (Kumar 1995). So while some members of the intelligentsia, metropolitan café-cultures and the 'art scene' may be in a position to indulge and celebrate difference and revolving identities, most others have to engage with the more monotonous aspects of modernity such as selling their labour power, caring for children and cleaning the house. So, old sources of identities such as class, gender and work are perhaps still crucial.

Authors such as Giddens and Beck prefer the term 'late modernity' (Beck 1992; Giddens 1990). For Giddens, belief in the truth of science, expert knowledge and reliable social systems has been eroded in the late modern period. A key outcome of this, according to Giddens, is that individuals no longer have 'ontological security' – ontology refers to the nature and essence of our being in the world. Giddens' term has similarities with Durkheim's notion of anomie (see Chapter 3) in that it refers to the consequences for individuals of becoming detached from their traditional moorings and thrown back on themselves to look for stability and meaning in their lives. We are now constantly faced with a range of choices and decisions about how we live in the world, for example the security of a 'job-for-life' can no longer be assumed, so people are losing a sense of being securely positioned in society. Late modernity is a period where dealing with, and continually reflecting upon, risk is now a central part of our lives. Indeed a short-hand term for late modern societies is 'risk society'. On his own website Giddens outlines succinctly what he means by this:

> Risk society is the term used to describe our modern society . . . The consequences of human actions on areas such as pollution, global warming, BSE, have introduced new sources of risk and uncertainty . . . In a risk society traditional certainties and securities can no longer be assumed. Increases in scientific knowledge lead to a more contingent society where the risks of anticipated events influence today's decisions. (Giddens 1999)

In another influential text, which deals with macro-level change, Beck (1992) also places risk at the centre of his discussion of the change from modernity to late modernity and the move from an industrial to a risk society. Beck's discussion parallels much of that of Giddens but he places a much bigger emphasis on global and ecological issues. He argues that the risks from pollution and climate change, for example, are now global and are not confined to particular nations. The 1986 Chernobyl disaster, the world's worst nuclear power accident (so far!), is a key event for Beck as it epitomised the way in which the effect of such ecological disasters cannot be contained within national borders but are global in consequence. In this sense, boundaries and frontiers dissolve and individual nation-states are losing their roles as organising forces in people's lives, particularly with the impact of globalisation (see below). Allied to this, Beck lists a range of social and economic changes such as contingent and insecure employment, the breakdown of the 'traditional family' and the rolling back of welfare-state provision. Within such a context, risk and uncertainty have become generalised throughout society and are a routine part of life for individuals.

Beck believes that 'individualisation' is now a key trait of our late modern times. This refers to the way in which individuals increasingly have to take responsibility for their own life, or biographies, and constantly have to make decisions to assess and re-assess the course of their life; they have, that is, to be reflexive. However, in order to be successful within such a risk society we may have to depend on the very social systems and expert knowledge that we have come to distrust. Think of the concerns over BSE and the mixed messages coming from the Government's food experts and the confusion over the interpretation of expert 'intelligence' on the existence of weapons of mass destruction in Iraq. Such episodes can shake our confidence in the institutions that we often depend on. Thus, living in a risk society can exert a heavy psychological toll on individuals.

GLOBALISATION

The world, it is often said, is becoming a smaller place. In many ways such a sentiment can be supported by prevailing economic and social trends in the world and the movement towards 'globalisation'. The term globalisation has a wide contemporary currency and has become something of an overused buzzword. Nevertheless, it is still worthy of discussion as it draws our attention to some social and economic processes that are said to be taking place in the world and which can have great consequences for us all. It is also an important concept in the writings of those such as Beck and Giddens.

For some time commentators have charted and analysed the development of global trade and the internationalisation of production (Frobel et al. 1980). Wallerstein (1983) has been writing about a 'world capitalist system' for over thirty years. Gargantuan companies, normally referred to as Trans National Corporations (TNCs), are the most obvious representations of the global economy. Companies, and brand names, such as Coca-Cola, Microsoft, Sony and others (you may want to try and think of some others) can seem omnipresent, if you ever travel around the globe. They certainly seem to transcend the national borders of their country of origin and are powerful symbols of a globalised world.

TNCs are vast organisations and dominate global production. The revenues of the top 500 global companies amount to over $11 trillion (a thousand billion), their assets exceeded $32 trillion and they employ around 35 million people (Sklair 2001). By way of comparison the combined GDP of New Zealand, Greece, Egypt, South Africa, Czech Republic and Israel was $540 billion in 1998 (Held and McGrew 2000). Indeed, of the largest 100 'economies' in the world 51 are global corporations and only 49 are countries. The huge economic, political and financial power of TNCs can render talk of *national* economies redundant. Similarly, other supranational organisations such as the World Bank, the EC, G7 and the International Monetary

Fund can also have the effect of diminishing the sovereignty of nation-states.

Some sectors of the UK economy, and thousands of jobs, are deeply integrated into the global economic system. The recent movement of UK call centres to Asia has highlighted the precarious nature of this 'dependency'. Over 10,000 jobs have been relocated to Asia (out of a UK total of 800,000) and this figure is expected to grow dramatically – in the US half a million jobs in the financial sector have been 'offshored', mainly to the Philippines and India (*Sunday Herald*, 30 November 2003). The major reason given for this is the ability to pay lower wages in these countries.

TNCs can also be seen as carriers of western culture and value systems and can contribute to a westernisation, and selling of particular 'lifestyles', to various localities around the globe. McDonald's, Microsoft, Levis, Nike and Starbucks are perhaps good illustrations of this. However, this can be resisted within certain regions and places as groups assert their identities and independence as they fight against global forces. So the impact of global forces can work out in particular ways within different localities; 'glocalisation' is the rather clumsy term coined to describe these interconnected processes between the local and the global (Beck 2000).

New technologies, such as satellite communication systems and the internet, have also had a huge impact in 'shortening' global time and distance. As a consequence it increasingly makes the world seem like a small place. Major sporting events such as the Olympics and the World Cup attract massive global audiences and for the duration of a football match a huge proportion of the world's population can be engaged in the same event – something that would have been unthinkable a couple of generations ago.

However, some writers warn us against exaggerating the importance of globalisation (Hirst and Thompson 1996). They insist that the international capitalist system has long been with us and contemporary processes of globalisation are, at most, merely a continuation of this expansionist trend. Others would argue against putting a positive gloss on globalisation as it often works out to the benefit of already rich and powerful nations and can accentuate already deeply entrenched global divisions (Cohen and Kennedy 2000).

As we have seen in this chapter an appreciation of social change is crucial for our sociological understanding of the world. The same can be said of an awareness of social divisions, to which we now turn.

FURTHER READING

Kumar, K. (1995), *From Post-industrial to Post-modern Society: New Theories of the Contemporary World*, Oxford: Blackwell. A readable discussion and critique of conceptions of post-industrialism and post-modernity.

Miles, S. (2001), *Social Theory in the Real World*, London: Sage. An excellent and engaged review of post-industrialism, post-modernity, globalisation, risk and other topics.

7 THE DIVIDED SOCIETY?

One of sociology's key concerns is the way in which 'society is divided into distinctive social groups, each uniting people through their particular and shared experiences and interests that mark them as different from, and possibly in conflict with, other groups' (Braham and Janes 2002: ix). Traditionally, sociology has always been interested in class as a major form of social division. Whilst class continues to be a much debated concept, it has been recognised that it is not the only factor in shaping social stratification, inequality and identity. Since the early 1970s sociologists became increasingly concerned with exploring, for example, gender and 'race' or ethnicity as key areas of social difference. More recently sociology has reflected wider interests in the study of age, disability, health, religion, nationality and sexuality.

IDENTITY AND DIFFERENCE

As we have already seen in Chapter 6, identity is the way we define ourselves in relation to others, and there are often multiple aspects to our identity. Take a moment to reflect on how you would describe yourself to someone if you were in a chat room on the internet. You can probably think of different ways of categorising yourself, perhaps along the lines of the film title *Single White Female*. You may refer to your gender, age, ethnicity, nationality, your job or where you live. These last two aspects may indicate your class to some extent, or at least other people will make some assumptions about your status and wealth on the basis of what you do and the location of your home.

Just as we categorise ourselves in particular ways, we also

place other people into different social groups: male/female; black/white; old/young; able-bodied/disabled; rich/poor. Our social characteristics identify us as being part of a group based on social divisions such as gender, class, ethnicity, age, sexuality, nationality and religion. As Braham and Janes point out: 'Everyone is included in the membership of these different groups and we make sense of our identities through our inclusion in some groups and exclusion from others' (2002: xi). Sociologists are interested in unpicking our stereotypical assumptions and questioning our taken-for-granted views of these social groupings. Within a group, all members are to some extent similar to one another, sharing certain experiences and interests. These shared characteristics bring them together and maintain them as a group, marking them off from others, perhaps creating a collective identity. Think for a moment about what the most important aspects of your individual and group identity are. How do social divisions shape the way you perceive yourself and the ways others perceive you?

We often make assumptions about people on the basis of these social categories, in the same way that others often judge us: 'Just as we pigeon-hole other people, and adapt our own behaviour towards them, so too do they adapt to us, in a continuing creative process' (Payne 2000a: 5). Hence, our perceptions of ourselves may change according to how others react to us because of how they perceive us at any given point in time. For example, one of the authors considers herself to be quite young, but when she does research with children and interviews 13–14-year-olds, they soon remind her that she is not young at all in their eyes. Particularly when they say things like 'oh, people of your generation do this . . .' or 'people your age think that . . .' In contrast, when she goes to play bridge at the local bridge club, she can soon be made to 'feel' young as most of the other players are over 60. So our identities and sense of self can change in relation to the people around us.

The categories of age, gender, class, ethnicity and so on are sociological 'labels' (Payne 2000a) and are not static or fixed. In other words, the ways in which we interpret these labels depends on how we have learnt to understand them in our society. Thus sociologists emphasise the socially constructed nature of such categories (see Chapter 3 for a discussion of social construction), that is, they may change over time and across different cultures. For example, gender roles have clearly changed over time. Two hundred years ago (see the novels of Jane Austen for a good example) the 'place' of women was very much perceived to be within the private sphere of the home, but nowadays it is more acceptable that women work in the public sphere and have careers. So gradually, through time, what can often appear to be natural and just the 'way of the world' – such as the relations between the genders – can be subject to change and transformation (see Chapter 6).

Similarly, the ways in which social divisions are interpreted vary in different cultures. For example, what it means to be poor in Britain is different from being poor in Asia. In the UK living in poverty may mean that a family lives in crammed conditions in poor-quality housing with no television but, in places like India, being very poor may mean not having enough food to eat and being in danger of dying of starvation. Hence, we cannot assume that the nature of poverty and the ways in which we understand wealth are constant over different cultures.

Thus, what it means to be rich or poor, male or female, young or old, black or white, and other potential sources of social division, are subject to variation. However, we should be careful not to exaggerate such changes as many social divisions remain relatively constant and resistant to rapid change. For example, although more women are working than in the past, they still tend to experience inequality in the workplace. Similarly when exploring generational relations we can see that, whilst in the last fifteen years children's rights have begun to be recognised, many parents still consider it acceptable to smack their children. The issue of physically disciplining children continues to be fiercely debated in Britain (Roberts 2000). Thus age-based ideas about adults having more power over children are likely to be resistant to change even though some notions, such as adult physical power, are being challenged. Consequently, the ways in which society is divided into groups can be ingrained in our particular cultural norms and values, thereby continuing to persist and only succumbing to gradual transformation. Social divisions are subject to both continuity and change and as sociologists we need to be aware of, and consider, both tendencies (see Chapter 6).

As an illustration of this, think about inequalities between men and women. Although, as we mentioned above, gender relations do vary, patterns of inequality can have a stubborn character. So, whilst many women have successful careers in the world of paid work, the number of women directors in the UK's top 100 firms (2001) has fallen for the third year in a row, 43 have no women on the board and only 2 per cent of executive directors are women (BBC 2001). In the English High Court and above, women make up just 7 per cent of the judiciary and currently only 23 per cent of Members of Parliament in the UK are women (NUS 2004).

Social divisions can directly affect the ways in which we interact with others on an everyday basis, even though we may not be constantly aware that our lives are structured by social inequalities and difference. For example, we may take for granted that we are part of a particular class, gender or age group, despite not having the time or inclination to think through the full implications of this. We are unlikely (sociology students excepted!) to continually relate our daily interactions and relations to wider social structures and will often consider ourselves to be individuals responsible for our own actions, rather than being shaped by our position within society.

You should stop and think for a moment about why you bought this book and how you came to consider going to university. Why are you studying at this point in your life? If you are a mature student, why did you not go to university five or ten years ago? What was it that stopped you going then and what has encouraged or enabled you to go now? Whatever your reason for studying at university level, you will probably think about what you have achieved as an individual. You will most likely have had to study hard to get the entrance requirements. In this sense, inequality can often appear to be down to individuals: what we have 'achieved' and what we have not. But have there been other factors working in your favour?

Inequality can often be conceptualised in highly individualistic terms, but inequality is also collective and shared. If some people do not go to university it may be because they are from a working-class background where their family expects, or needs, them to leave school at the earliest opportunity and get a job rather than continue studying. Thus, going into higher education may be the result of a range of social factors rather than being merely the consequence of individual choices and actions. Children from wealthier families are more likely to benefit from good health, achieve educational success and gain well-paid employment than those born into poverty. Our social positioning shapes the opportunities and constraints which we experience throughout our lives but as individuals we do not often question this process. As sociologists we should (see Chapter 3 for a discussion of the relation between 'agency' and 'structure').

In other words then, we do not exist only as individuals. In fact, we cannot exist in isolation, we are dependent on each other in various ways and we live within a social context. Our life chances and our actions are subsequently shaped by the social and as sociologists we need to take this into account. Social divisions based around gender, age, ethnicity, nationality, religion, sexuality and disability affect our individual life chances because rewards and privileges are unevenly distributed often according to which of these 'divisions' we may find ourselves in. Consequently, our lifestyle may be constrained or enhanced in relation to our social location. The rest of this section considers the ways in which society is structured by social divisions and how these are sustained over time, often resulting in social inequalities.

POWER AND INEQUALITY

Sociologists are interested in social divisions because they reflect the ways in which different societies are structured and organised. A key issue is how to define the labels given to these sources of division. This can lead to asking questions such as what *is* class and what *is* gender? We need to think carefully about how these social divisions have emerged and what their key characteristics are. For example, on what basis do we separate out the, very British, categories of upper, middle and working class? This can be done hierarchically on the basis of perceived social difference which can reflect the imbalances of power (Payne 2000a). Consequently, the study of social divisions is often linked to exploring social disadvantage as when one group is advantaged this can impact negatively upon other groups.

We also need to ask, how are such social divisions maintained over time? Taking the example of class again: why do working-class people rarely become part of the upper class? Why is it difficult for poor people to become rich? There are of course exceptions and some individuals can achieve a high degree of social mobility, but why is it that generally we stay within the class we are born into? A combination of both power and ideology can lead to the persistence of patterns of inequality, and we shall look briefly at each of these in turn.

Sociologists have a keen interest in power (Lukes 1974) as they strive to explore and explain processes of domination and subordination. Bauman and May comment that:

> Some people enjoy a wider range of choice due to their access to more resources and we can refer to this in terms of *power*. Power is best understood as pursuing freely chosen ends towards which our actions are oriented and of then commanding the necessary means towards the pursuit of those ends. Power, therefore, is an enabling capacity. (Bauman and May 2001: 62)

When social groups are arranged in a hierarchy, some form of power is being exercised. If certain characteristics of a group are perceived to be valued more highly than others, that group can become more powerful relative to others. However, power involves the ability to put your actions and ideas into practice and in order to do that you need to be able to persuade others of your superiority. For power to be effective, people must believe that you can exercise that power. For example, for adult power to be effective, children have to believe that adults will discipline them, that the power of adults will be exercised.

Social divisions do not just involve unequal power relations but also beliefs about those power relations. In this way power is linked to ideology, which can be usefully defined as: 'Shared ideas or beliefs which serve to justify the interests of dominant groups' (Giddens 2001: 691). The meanings we attach to social differences are important in the way we use them to justify why such divisions exist:

> Social divisions are not random, because they are normally rooted in positions of power and advantage, where those blessed with both of these define themselves as 'above' those who do not share their particular advantages or the attributes associated with them, such as ways of speaking, mode of dress and other symbols of personal and group identity. (Bilton et al. 2002: 71)

Groups with more power have a greater ability to maintain their status, which is rooted in their advantaged position. For example, the 'upper class' can sustain its position by reflecting its class advantage in its accent, table manners, clothes and other signifiers of its status and 'position'. The most privileged and powerful groups in society have the most to gain from maintaining existing social structures and arrangements, whilst those with fewer social resources are more likely to try to resist them, seek change or perhaps resign themselves to doing nothing. For the more disadvantaged groups, social divisions can be constraining but, for the advantaged groups, they can be enabling. It is often those who are more privileged in society that have the power to maintain these distinctions, which is why, as the old adage goes, the 'rich tend to get richer whilst the poor get poorer' (see Reid 1998). Therefore, we need to think about both the opportunities and constraints of social divisions.

One of the key consequences of social divisions is that the unequal power relations between groups often result in social inequalities. Some groups have a greater share of resources, which can enable them to have more control over their lives. When we talk about resources we are not just referring to access to money but also access to, for example, good health, education and a range of leisure pursuits. There are two basic types of inequality. The most obvious is material inequality which relates to economic inequalities between people, including wealth and income. The second form is symbolic inequality which involves less tangible qualities such as status, power and respect (Sennet 2004). As we have seen, some people are 'valued' more highly than others and may have greater control over improving their life chances. As Payne explains:

> [S]ocial divisions tend to divide people into 'better' or 'worse' categories . . . Those in the 'better' categories have more control over their own lives, usually more money, and can generally be seen to lead happier lives. Those occupying the better positions often take their advantages for granted, but nonetheless, social divisions are still all about advantage and disadvantage. They are therefore also about who has the *power* to create and maintain this situation in which inequalities persist. (Payne 2000a: 4)

Given this, key concepts which you will come across in sociology include marginalisation, social exclusion and discrimination. Bilton et al. define social exclusion as 'The ways in which people are marginalised from society by having limited or no access to public services, and little participation in education and the political process' (2002: 81). One of the main roles of sociologists is to understand social differences and try to explain social inequalities. This, in turn, can help policy-makers try to minimise the negative treatment of those on the margins of society. For example, in relation to age, children and older people in the UK are those most likely to be socially excluded as they have less access to social resources, such as wealth, power and status. Britain is an overtly ageist society and we tend to marginalise certain age groups, especially the very young and the very old. Thus age is a social division which can create, and maintain, inequality and difference (Bradley 1996).

As we have discussed above, we can have multiple aspects to our identity. Additionally, different social divisions can interconnect in complex ways. For example, consider how age intersects with gender and class: the life experience of a young middle-class male will be very different to that of an older working-class female. As Braham and Janes point out, 'We are all a complex amalgam of multiple aspects of identity and members of several different socially divided groups . . . Social divisions often connect and overlap in ways that reinforce disadvantage, but can also operate in contradictory ways' (2002: xii).

Thus, we need to consider the ways in which social divisions intersect. For example, black feminists argued strongly that there is not a unified women's experience (hooks 1986). Women may share a gender identity to some extent but there is also much inequality between women. A middle-class white woman may employ a black working-class woman as her nanny, so that she can afford to go out to work and be independent. Thus people may be similar in one context but different in another.

Furthermore, it is important to take a worldview and be able to recognise that what happens in our society, or even in other western societies, is not necessarily the norm. Sociologists are keen to consider global divisions in terms of both social and economic inequalities between different world areas. Think for a moment about your own privileged position in global terms. If you are at university or are planning to go, you are likely not only to have had better access to education but also to basic services such as electricity, drinking water and decent housing compared with most of the global population. A sociological perspective, then, should remind us that many of our achievements that we attribute to our personal abilities are also products of the privileged position which we hold within the global social system. Therefore, social divisions take place at two different levels: within a particular society as well across different societies.

The process of social differentiation may be a universal feature of human societies but it should be understood as a dynamic process which changes over time and across particular cultures. Thus, the ways in which societies are unequal vary from one culture to another. For example, in more traditional pre-industrial societies, social differentiation may be based mainly on gender and age. Whereas in more complex societies, social differentiation may arise as a consequence of a wider range of factors, many of which we have discussed above.

In summary, social divisions are an important part of our identities but tend to result in social inequalities. Social divisions persist and are reproduced over time, yet they also are subject to gradual change. Several key features of social divisions include the following (adapted from Payne 2000b: 242):

- A principle of social organisation

- Long-lasting but not fixed

- Sustained by ideologies, institutions and interactions

- Involves unequal opportunities of access to resources

- Produces shared social identities

- Feature of human societies

Thus we hope that sociology will enable you to raise questions about how you view yourself and others. It may encourage you to reflect on your own social identity and the ways in which you categorise yourself and other people as young or old, rich or poor, male or female. Sociology also reminds us that our life chances and our experiences of the social world differ dramatically according to what location within a particular society we are born into.

AGE AS A SOCIAL DIVISION

In this last section we provide a more detailed discussion of age (drawn from Punch forthcoming 2005) so that you can see the kinds of issues that could be explored in relation to any social division such as class, gender, ethnicity, disability and so on.

Age as a social construction

For a long time age has divided societies by distinguishing one group of people from another but, apart from some notable exceptions (such as Eisenstadt 1956), age has only recently become a topic for sociologists (Bradley 1996). In the past it has been assumed that ageing is a biological process that 'naturally' affects everyone. Now it is recognised that age is also socially determined and that our experiences of age can depend on the society we live in. Different cultures attach a range of meanings and values to different age groups, and this affects the ways we behave as well as how we treat others.

Sometimes our age may inhibit us from doing certain things, and, at other times, we are able to behave in particular ways because of how old we are. Thus, age can be both enabling and constraining. Our age may influence where we shop, what we buy and even how we pay for goods. For example, older people may prefer to pay by cheque, younger people may be more used to using Maestro or visa cards and children may use cash as they are less likely to have access to bank accounts.

Our age may affect the types of books we read, the music we listen to, the television programmes we watch, the leisure activities we engage in. Thus our everyday lives are shaped to a certain extent by the way our age is understood and expressed in the society we live in.

Ideas about age-appropriate behaviour are socially constructed rather than based solely on biology. For example, what children can or cannot do tends to reflect their 'social age' rather than their 'biological age'. An eight-year-old can smoke: it is biologically possible but socially it is considered to be inappropriate for a person of that age. Usually it is adults, parents, policy-makers or lawyers, who decide what children are allowed to do at different ages largely because we perceive children to be immature, vulnerable and in need of protection. Thus the age at which people can drink alcohol, have sex, smoke or drive is often not based on their physical or mental abilities but rather on what society deems to be appropriate. These age-based norms are maintained by ideologies which are resistant to rapid change but can change gradually over time.

Age and identity

Societies are structured and organised by age in a variety of ways. For example, age is used as a basis for group membership for certain institutions, such as school, nurseries and youth clubs. Some age-based organisations for children are also gendered, so boys go to Cubs then Scouts when they are older, whereas girls go to Brownies then Guides. Consequently, children are separated off from much of the adult social world by spending a large part of their lives in age-related contexts. In such ways children develop an understanding of 'appropriate' age relationships and build up knowledge of the ways in which the world is structured through age. They learn about power and authority by seeing the different status that is given to adults and children.

Therefore, involvement in age-based institutions can create a sense of identity with those of a particular generation. People of a similar age share a common historical experience and may develop a sense of social solidarity and togetherness. This can be reinforced by consumer goods such as music and clothes which are targeted at certain generations. Some fashions are perceived to be exclusive to specific age categories and tend to transmit age-related messages. Attitudes can also mark off generations as being different from one another. Certain attitudes can be perceived as 'old-fashioned' and out-dated, particularly when you hear older people talking about things that happened 'in their day'. Thus, as Vincent argues, 'Generation is a cultural phenomenon; a set of symbols, values and practices which not only endure but unfold as a cohort ages' (2003: 115–16).

Age, power and inequality

As we have seen, age stratification involves the unequal distribution of social resources, including wealth, power and status, which are accorded to people on the basis of their age. As Victor suggests, 'Every society divides individuals into age groups or strata and this stratification reflects and creates age-related differences in capacities, roles, rights and privileges' (1994: 39). Thus key age groupings in our society are childhood, youth, young adulthood, mid-life and old age (Bradley 1996). In British society, the two ends of the life course, childhood and old age, tend to illustrate the ways in which we attach less value and status to some age groups compared to others.

In the UK, both children and older people lack power, autonomy and independence in relation to the more dominant social category of adults. Children and older people are often perceived as being dependent on adults, in need of care and vulnerable. They tend to be seen as reliant on others, sometimes described as burdens. Furthermore, they are often treated as if they are unable to speak for themselves. Their voices are silenced as adults take over and tend to speak on their behalf. For example, during a visit to a health clinic parents tend to discuss their child's illness with the doctor rather than allowing the child to speak directly for themselves. Similarly, at a residential care home, the adult son or daughter is often likely to speak to the care staff on behalf of his or her older parent who is resident.

Age and discrimination

People can be discriminated against, or negatively stereotyped, because of their age and this is known as 'ageism'. As Vincent points out: 'Ageism, like racism or sexism, refers to both prejudice and discrimination; the first being an attitude, the second a behaviour' (2000: 148). Older people tend to suffer from ageism more than other age groups, as the process of ageing is often perceived with fear. We only have to look at the slogans on birthday cards to see the stigma attached to growing older. However, people of all ages can experience negative treatment because of their age: 'ageism places limits, constraints and expectations at *every* stage from birth on-wards' (Johnson and Bytheway 1993: 204). Consequently, we need to remember that ageism is not just directed at older people.

This example of age as a social division illustrates many of the key issues (social construction, identity, power, inequality and discrimination) which can be involved in processes of social differentiation. It is also worth bearing in mind that social differences and divisions can lead to social conflict and social problems, as discussed in the next chapter.

FURTHER READING

Bradley, H. (1996), *Fractured Identities: Changing Patterns of Inequality*, Cambridge: Polity. This book explores four key social divisions: class, gender, age and ethnicity, illustrating the dynamic ways in which they interact.

Braham, P. and Janes, L. (eds) (2002), *Social Differences and Divisions*, Oxford: Blackwell. This is an accessible introduction to social differences, which not only considers class, gender and race, but also explores citizenship, social justice, education and housing.

Payne, G. (ed.) (2000), *Social Divisions*, London: Macmillan. This book provides an excellent overview of many key social divisions, including class, gender, ethnicity, nationality, age, sexuality, disability, health and community.

8 THE PROBLEMATIC SOCIETY?

A large part of the impetus behind the development of sociology was the desire to understand the transformations that were taking place within certain societies. The nature of 'order' and the consequences of social change were among the key concerns of the early sociologists. Society and all its attendant problems, actual or potential, have been of interest to sociologists ever since.

When we consider what is 'problematic' in any society, at any particular time, we imply a notion of how the world 'should be': of what could be described as 'normal social functioning'. What is 'normal' is no less difficult to define as what is seen to be a 'problem' and can involve us in normative discussions about society, that is, moral judgements about the way the world 'should be'. This is not necessarily a bad thing, but we should be wary about imposing our own personal view of the world. In addition, sociologists should avoid explaining, or justifying, events or conditions in the social world by asserting that this is just the 'way things are' or it is 'only natural'.

As we have argued, to think sociologically is to emphasise the socially constructed and historically specific nature of the human-made world (Jenkins 2002) and events and phenomenon within that world. This means that what is seen to be problematic (and of course normal) changes over time and varies across different cultures and it is crucial to bear this in mind if we are to think sociologically about these issues. The social world may appear fixed and given at times; however, sociology can help us to reflect upon its often fragile and contested nature.

There are many examples of activities that were once seen to be problematic which are taken to be normal nowadays – you should try to think of some. For example, drinking tea – once known as 'scandalbroth' – was associated with debauchery and gossip mongering in seventeenth-century Britain. The very idea of women voting in national elections was seen to be utterly bizarre by most men (and many women, it has to be said) in the early part of the twentieth century and, during the same time period, smoking tobacco was portrayed as being an invigorating and fortifying activity. Attitudes towards sex and sexuality have undergone numerous changes and reinterpretations, as have those relating to taking drugs. Alcohol consumption is prohibited in some countries and is legal in others. We could go on.

So, when we think about social problems we should ask questions such as: why is it a problem? Who is it a problem for? Who is telling us that it is a problem? When did it emerge as a problem? Agreeing upon what constitutes a social problem is not an easy matter (May et al. 2001). It gets more complicated when we consider that problems can be understood as an opportunity for some. For example, the existence of widespread poverty could provide opportunities for a whole range of money lenders; unemployment can benefit employers by dampening down demands for pay increases and the 'crime problem' can of course keep thousands of police officers in jobs!

GEMEINSCHAFT AND GESELLSCHAFT

Very often the perceived problematic nature of societies, at any particular time, is contrasted with the way 'things used to be'. 'It wasn't like this twenty years ago' is a common refrain that you may be familiar with and may inevitably recant yourself one day! (Pearson 1983). Pearson satires such sentiments when discussing street crime and the myth of the British 'way of life' and how it now seems that, 'The streets of Britain have been suddenly plunged into an unnatural state of disorder that betrays the stable traditions of the past.' He goes on to say that, 'what I hope to show by contrast is that real traditions are quite different: that for generations Britain has been plagued by the same fears and problems as today' (Pearson 1983: ix). We do not have to agree with Pearson to recognise the point being made.

The contrast between a problematic present and a more harmonious past was formalised over a hundred years ago by the German sociologist Ferdinand Tonnies (1855–1936) in his influential dichotomy, *Gemeinschaft* and *Gesellschaft* (community and society). This is a model of social forms that Tonnies did not think actually existed in reality but was useful for gauging how far we may have changed from one to the other. Briefly, *Gemeinschaft* (community) is characterised by the following: integrated small-scale communities, social relations which are long-lasting and multi-faceted and a culture of collectivity. Whereas *Gesellschaft* (society) has the following traits: industrial/urbanised settings, the dominance of money transactions and the marketplace, relations between people are impersonal, fleeting and individualistic. This distinction crops up a lot in discussions about the problems associated with the present and it is something you will come across regularly when reading your way through the sociological literature.

PRIVATE TROUBLES AND PUBLIC ISSUES

In his celebrated text *The Sociological Imagination* (1959), Wright Mills makes a distinction between 'personal troubles' and 'public issues' which has proved to be of lasting influence (see Loney et al. 1991). As Wright Mills puts it:

> Perhaps the most fruitful distinction with which the sociological imagination works is between 'the personal troubles of the milieu' and 'the public issues of social structure'. This distinction is an essential tool of the sociological imagination and a feature of all classic work in social science. (1959: 14)

Personal troubles are primarily to do with the self and personal biography and the source of the trouble is to be found in the particular character and/or the lifestyle of the individual. Such a trouble is a private matter, located and resolved within the immediate context. In contrast, public issues are matters that transcend biography and the local context and can relate to institutions and social structures. The remedy to such issues is generally seen to be beyond the remedy of a single person and involve a situation where widely held values are threatened. In this sense public issues are *social* problems.

Wright Mills' distinction is useful when we reflect on the manner in which a personal trouble becomes, or is seen to be, a public issue or a social problem. As an illustration, consider growing concerns over obesity in many countries, including the UK. Is this to be considered a problem solely explicable in terms of the eating and lifestyle habits of a particular person (or persons)? Or does the apparent increasing levels of obesity in a society necessitate a larger collective response? Can we just hope that millions of individuals will take measures to deal with their personal obesity problem or should the state and the government step in to tackle the problem at a national level? For example, should the government provide health warnings and tax fatty, high calorie foods? Similar issues are raised when we think about smoking-related illnesses. Other examples we could consider in a similar way are the causes and remedies for poverty and unemployment.

It is important to note that it is not just a question of scale or numbers which determines whether something is a personal trouble or a public issue. Some may argue that despite millions of people living in poverty, dying of AIDS or being unemployed it is still their own personal trouble and up to them to resolve any situation they find themselves in. Thus, it may not be seen as a *legitimate* social problem – that is, something that the state will become involved in. So the process whereby personal troubles become public issues can be complex and is often contested. As Wright Mills says, 'An issue is a public matter: [when] some value cherished by publics is felt to be threatened' (1959: 8). We will discuss some examples below.

Durkheim argues that we inhabit a moral universe, 'moral' in the widest sense of the forms of solidarity which can bind us together and make society a recognisable whole that we feel part of. If some thing, event or person(s) is seen to threaten this fragile moral entity then a state of anomie (see Chapter 3) can ensue. A legitimate social problem may emerge along with a strong sense that something 'should be done' to rectify the situation and restore order and equilibrium (Jamrozik and Nocella 1998).

We have seen from the discussion of the 'Divided Society' (Chapter 7) that power within a society is not evenly distributed. Thus we should ask *whose* values are under threat and from where is this claim being made (Jamrozik and Nocella 1998). Howard Becker used the term 'moral entrepreneurs', in his now classic text *Outsiders* (1973), to draw attention to the way that certain individuals can have their understanding of what constitutes a social problem heard above others. Moral entrepreneurs are seen to have a legitimate voice and opinion in a way that more marginalised and less powerful groups and individuals do not. Those with social power and capital can often have their definition of events upheld and an ability to influence agendas, enforce rules, define problems and impose their 'solutions'.

We do not need to be an advocate of 'conspiracy theories' to argue that in a society such as the UK there are concentrations of power, wealth and privilege (Reid 1998). It is also the case that dominant groups are in a position to have their ideas and values seen to be the norm for all of society – Marxists would describe such a group as a 'ruling class'. In this respect the media can play an important role in selecting which issues get discussed as well as setting the parameters and rules of engagement for any subsequent debates – although it is worth noting that powerful people and groups exerted such an influence long before the advent of TV, mass-circulation newspapers and the internet! Of course there is never a totally dominant worldview but it can amount to a powerful hegemony, to use a term normally associated with the Italian social thinker Antonio Gramsci (1891–1937) (see Bocock 1986).

This is a term that points to a diffusion of values, beliefs and morals through society that tend to be supportive of the established order of that society and prevailing inequalities of power.

We can think about current debates and panics about 'anti-social' behaviour and 'ned' culture. It is almost bizarre to imagine a situation where those who are labelled 'neds' (normally young and relatively poor individuals) are given an equal opportunity to explain their behaviour or their account of events – and would they be listened to if they did? The less powerful in society have less resources and less social and economic capital to set moral agendas and to make decisions about what, and who, are seen to be social problems. Certainly there is a long history in this country of powerful people passing judgement on the less powerful and finding their behaviour to be problematic in some sense (see Smith 2002). Generally there are a whole range of potentially problematic behaviours and events within the social world and they do not all have the status of a legitimate social problem, or they may have only recently been thought of in this way. A good example is domestic violence, which only relatively recently in the UK has been seen to be a social problem in which the police could legitimately intervene. Prior to the 1970s it tended to be perceived as a private, individual family problem (Morgan 1985).

MORAL PANICS

Stanley Cohen dealt with similar issues in his classic book *Folk Devils and Moral Panics: The Creation of the Mods and Rockers* (2002), from which the term 'moral panic' has gained widespread currency. Cohen argues that societies are subject to periods of instability when a particular event(s) or group of people are perceived to threaten certain values and this results in a collective response. Schematically we could say that moral panics go through the following stages:

A Warning: this may take the form of 'threatening' behaviour, symbols of deviance and difference (such as hair, clothes, demeanour and so on). Threats to order or cherished values are established and a 'folk devil(s)' may emerge.

An Impact: particular events and/or episodes are amplified through the media.

Inventory: a period of 'taking stock' may occur. This will involve the marshalling of 'expert opinion' and explanation from government ministers, academics and assorted experts. A strong belief that 'something should be done' emerges.

Reaction: an attempt at recovery and restoration. A state response can follow, perhaps resulting in the passage of new laws. (Adapted from Cohen 2002)

At the heart of a moral panic there is normally an actual event that may have terrible consequences for those people involved (football violence for example, with 'hooligans' being the 'folk devils') and this should not be overlooked. However, the point about a moral panic is that the reaction to a particular episode or 'folk devil(s)' is out of all proportion to the actual harm that results, or could ever possibly result. A good example of this would be the recurring moral panics in relation to welfare benefit fraud (threats to the values of work and the 'work ethic'), teenage pregnancies (threats to 'family values') and current anxieties over asylum seekers (threats to a 'British way of life'). In these cases the level of media coverage and actual resources diverted to these issues can seem out of proportion to the reality of the threat or problem involved. There are, conversely, glaring silences about other issues. For example, the amount of money involved in benefit fraud is considerably less than the amount lost to the exchequer through tax evasion. However, moral panics over tax evasion are noticeable by their absence and there is relatively little effort put into trying to reduce it (Cook 1989).

In the wake of some moral panics there can be significant changes to the law. Moral panics about 'mugging' in the 1970s resulted in new 'stop-and-search' powers for the police. The Criminal Justice and Public Order Act (1994), which changed the law on trespass and criminal damage, was introduced after moral panics about 'new age travellers' and 'raves' – both of which involved tiny numbers of individuals but threatened cherished values relating to private property and access to the land (Hall et al. 1978; Hetherington 2000)

THINKING ABOUT CRIME

There are a range of social problems which we can look at from a sociological perspective. Poverty, unemployment and racism are just three examples from a much longer list we could choose from. Lack of space will confine us to a closer look at one perennial social problem which has been the focus of a great deal of sociological work, that of crime. We shall also discuss the closely related notion of deviance.

Crime is generally regarded as a major social problem in many societies. You may have already guessed that trying to define crime is extremely difficult given that what is understood as crime (and deviance) varies across societies and over time. Thus there is no universal definition of crime or criminal behaviour to which we can refer. Deviance is generally a broader concept than crime and can best be described as behaviour that veers from what is regarded as being normal at any particular moment, with all the attendant problems of definition that this brings. Deviant behaviour is not necessarily 'bad' or criminal of course and may be understood as being eccentric or bizarre – consider someone who insists on walking around barefoot in rain-swept Edinburgh! You can also be 'criminal' and not deviant. For example, in some contexts it would be seen as 'normal' not to return the extra pound you received in your change when you bought a round of drinks; you may well be regarded as deviant if you did.

Crime also impacts differentially on people. You are much

more likely to be violently attacked if you are a male under 25, than a woman over 75. You are also more likely to have your house burgled if you live in a depressed socio-economic area rather than a wealthy one. As with other social problems such as poverty, unemployment and ill-health, the problem of crime is more of a problem for some than it is for others. As mentioned above, it is both a problem *and* an opportunity for the likes of lawyers, judges, prison officers and some politicians. Given these issues of definition and impact you can anticipate that the measurement of crime, as represented by 'crime rates' for example, is somewhat problematic – an issue we will return to below.

Criminality is often discussed as if it was an attribute belonging to a particular type of personality, as though it was the preserve of an entirely separate group of individuals. Now, some forms of crime such as violent murders are thankfully very rare, but the whole range of criminal activities from fraud to embezzlement to stealing and property damage is much more common and widespread and generally not best understood as being the preserve of some kind of 'criminal type'. To illustrate this we can borrow from Muncie and McLaughlin (1996) and ask you to consider if you have done any of the following:

- Bought goods knowing they have been stolen

- Kept the money when you receive too much change

- Taken 'souvenirs' from a pub or hotel

- Left a shop without paying in full for your purchases

- Watched a television without a licence

Under the law these are all regarded as punishable offences. The maximum penalty for watching a television without a licence is £1,000, for the rest you *could* be (unlikely as it is) imprisoned for up to six months (for a fuller account see

Muncie and McLaughlin 1996). We will leave it to you to ponder over your involvement, if any, in this list. The point of this exercise is not to make you feel like a 'criminal', on the basis of the above it is doubtful that you would 'see' yourself as one anyway. However, it allows us to highlight the ways in which much criminality, certainly of this more 'petty' nature, is *not* so detached from us as we may like to think. Crossing over into illegality is very common for many of us and at a social level could even be described as 'normal'.

A hundred years ago, Émile Durkheim famously described crime in just this way. For him crime is present in all types of societies and as he says:

> Everywhere and always there have been [people] who have conducted themselves in such a way as to bring down punishment on their heads . . . crime is normal because it is completely impossible for any society entirely free of it to exist. (Durkheim 1982: 98–9)

Durkheim was not condoning crime ('excessiveness is pathological') but was pointing out that a certain level of criminality was normal for any social formation. It could even serve a useful social function in as much that as criminals or deviants break rules they could force some people to reassess what is normal and contribute to social change. Crime and the punishment of crime could also spell out clearly to those within a particular society what was 'wrong' and what was 'right'. As Durkheim brilliantly puts it, 'Crime brings together honest men and concentrates them' (quoted in Giddens 1972: 127).

'EXPLAINING' CRIME

Explanations of crime are almost as old as crime itself. Biological accounts try to explain crime through some kind of genetic predisposition to 'break the law'. Such notions of 'pathological' individuals are still powerful at a popular level – think of comments about 'dodgy'- or 'shifty'-*looking* individuals. Psychological accounts may place the emphasis on traumatic experiences in childhood that can lead to a 'career' in crime. The individual may have some form of 'mental illness' or a range of 'personality problems' such as impulsiveness or irritability which can underlie their move into criminality. Sociologists would tend not to 'explain' crime and criminality (or deviance) from any of these starting points, and would be likely to take issue, not to say exception, with all of them.

Sociologists ask different questions when thinking about the 'social problem' of crime. The very category 'crime' would be problematised to begin with. As discussed above, what constitutes crime changes with time and place. Do we equate it with 'breaking the law'? But what is the status of all those acts that people 'commit' which are not detected by the law enforcement agencies – all those people watching TV without a licence for example? Can we commit a crime even though we do not get caught? If that is so, then the 'actual' crime rate, or the level of 'hidden' crime, would be incalculably huge. In addition, as we alluded to above, legal definitions of crime change and are not fixed or given. This makes it problematic to compare levels of crime across different societies and different time periods.

Durkheim has had a lasting influence on sociological accounts of crime. He used the term 'conscience collective' (or 'common conscience') to describe the moral regulative force that exists in society to help bind individuals together. This he defines as the 'totality of beliefs and sentiments common to the average members of a society' (Durkheim 1984: 38–9). For Durkheim, a criminal act is so defined if it offends this conscience collective. As he puts it, 'We must not say that an action shocks the common conscience because it is criminal but rather that it is criminal *because* it shocks the common conscience' (1984: 39, our emphasis). This is important as Durkheim is suggesting that there is nothing *inherent* in the act itself that can define it as being criminal but it is the social *reaction* to it that defines it as such, and this reaction will differ from society to society and change over time.

Thus we should think of crime less as an objective category or 'fact' but as something having strong subjective, or normative, elements. We should, in essence, emphasise the socially constructed nature of crime. This is not to say that the consequence of criminal activity cannot be devastating for individuals; of course it can. However, it highlights the way that crime exists within strong moral codes of right and wrong, and these can shift and change within societies. We can best understand crime through an awareness of the social context within which the activity takes place. To illustrate this, consider someone plunging a knife into another person's chest. This could be done by a surgeon, as the consequence of fighting in a war or during a violent attack on the street, or be the result of a freak accident or self-defence. In each case the context gives a different meaning to the activity, which on its own tells us very little.

Durkheim's insights into crime and deviance proved influential to later generations of sociologists, particularly those who developed 'labelling theory'. This was mostly associated with the sociology of deviance and focused on the social reaction to a particular group or individual. As Becker (who is closely associated with this approach) states:

> Social groups create deviance by making the rules whose infraction constitutes deviance, and by applying those rules to particular people and labelling them outsiders. From this point of view deviance is not a quality of the act a person commits . . . The deviant is one to whom that label has been applied; deviant behaviour is behaviour that people so label. (Becker 1973: 9)

So labelling theory takes away the emphasis from the activity, or event, and places it on the reaction. It also makes us think about *rule-makers* as well as rule-breakers. We have already discussed Becker's moral entrepreneur who has the ability to make and uphold rules that people may break. This is referred to in the following, oft-quoted, passage:

Before any act can be viewed as deviant, and before any class of people can be labelled and treated as outsiders for committing the act, someone must have made the rule which defines the act as deviant. Rules are not made automatically. (Becker 1973: 162)

Again this makes us think about relations of power within society and who has the ability to make labels 'stick' to certain groups (for some criticisms of this approach see Croall 1998).

MEASURING CRIME

Many of the problems associated with the quantification of phenomena in the social world are highlighted when we consider the measurement of crime. As we mentioned above, 'hidden crime' (those infringements of the law that are never detected and processed) only adds to the problem of assessing the level of crime in any society. As Fattah says, 'it is utterly impossible to know the actual number of criminal offences and law violations committed by all members of a given community' (1997: 95).

Crime rates and other statistics used to measure and represent crime can be usefully understood as social constructions. Rather than seeing them as hard evidence and measurements, set down in precise percentages and presented via impressive graphs, tables and charts, we need to think about the social processes that take place 'underneath' these stark statistics and numbers (Fattah 1997; Pearson 1983). Decisions have to be made about what is a crime (and what is not), how will this be recorded (or not) and whether a particular police force has the people-power to record and investigate every case that is brought to its attention.

At a more general level, it could be argued that the legal justice system in the UK (the police, the courts, the prison service and so on) functions, in the main, to process young working-class men – a look at the make-up of prison populations will confirm this. It could be that this reflects the kinds of

people who break the law most but it could also be a consequence of the fact that a whole range of other social groups
do not fall under its 'gaze'.

Sociologists have brought other types of crime into focus
such as 'white-collar crime', 'corporate crime' and the crimes
of the powerful such as 'state crime' (Croall 1998). In contrast
to 'conventional crime', these other forms of crime are carried
out by relatively powerful individuals, organisations and
agencies. Examples would include the deaths of thousands
of individuals due to the release of poisonous gases into the air
by an unscrupulous multinational company; the many thousands of people killed and injured at work due to companies
not meeting their legal requirements to maintain health and
safety standards; and the huge number of those who may die
as a consequence of a state declaring an illegal war on another
state. These actions can make us radically rethink what crime
is and view it as being, in part, a consequence of what is *seen* as
a 'crime problem' and who are routinely thought of as
potential criminals. Thus, perhaps there is more than one
crime problem and crime statistics represent the selective
nature as to what counts as crime.

We are emphatically *not* suggesting that quantitative approaches are of no value. They are of course invaluable, but
we have to be aware that such 'facts' and figures are the
outcome of social process and this should be borne in mind.
This is particularly useful to think about when we try to
compare the crime rates of different societies and across
different time periods. What is understood to constitute criminality changes, sometimes radically, between different cultures and over time. So we should be sceptical, for example,
about claims that the 'crime rate' is five, ten or fifteen times
'worse' now than it was in the 1890s or 1930s or that other
societies are much more crime-free than ours.

In Parts II and III of this book we have demonstrated that
developing a sociological imagination can enable us to both
theorise and investigate the various forms of social problems
and social divisions that exist within society as well as making
us perceptive to processes of social change. By showing some

of the ways sociology can enable us to understand the contemporary world, hopefully we have confirmed that your decision to study sociology is a good one. The final part of the book will give you some ideas about the practical skills required for studying sociology at university.

FURTHER READING

May, M., Page, R. and Brunsdon, E. (eds) (2001), *Understanding Social Problems: Issues in Social Policy*, Oxford: Blackwell. A good introduction to the study of social problems and includes discussions of crime, poverty and domestic violence.

Croall, H. (1998), *Crime and Society in Britain*, London: Longman. A comprehensive and clearly written introduction to the study of crime.

Cohen, S. (2002) [1972], *Folk Devils and Moral Panics: The Creation of the Mods and Rockers*, 3rd edn, London: Routledge. A sociological classic which remains an engaging and thought-provoking read. The third edition has a very useful new introductory chapter.

PART IV
Study Skills

The first three parts of this book have encouraged you to think about the subject matter of sociology and the aim of this part is to help prepare you for studying sociology at university. To this end, we provide an overview of the range of study skills students should gain at university, including how to get the most out of lectures, workshops and reading. It also gives practical guidance on writing sociology essays and exam preparation.

9 STUDYING AT UNIVERSITY

The biggest difference between university and school is that you are now largely responsible for your own learning. Lecturers and tutors are there to help and guide you, but the main emphasis is on you to develop your own effective learning strategies. This book will point you in the right direction, but you will need to recognise that hard work on your part is required during your degree. The good news is that since you have chosen to do sociology then you will find most of what you do interesting and engaging – we hope! This part of the text aims to take some of the worry out of daily life at university.

University can open up great opportunities so aim to make the most of it. At school it is often assumed to be 'cool' not to be perceived to be working too hard, but at university you no longer need to play those games. Your future life and career could be affected by your degree and the grade you achieve – do your best and do not leave yourself with any doubt about whether you could have done better if you had tried harder. What do you want to get out of the university experience? Hopefully it is not just purely about getting a qualification, but also about a desire to stretch the boundaries of your knowledge and question the way the world works. We think sociology will help you achieve this. The more time and effort you put into studying, the more you will be rewarded, so, in a nutshell, get stuck in!

THE COURSE OUTLINE AND DEPARTMENT HANDBOOK

Most courses have a course outline with essential information such as the lecture and workshop programme, reading lists

and the assessment requirements. In addition, most departments have an undergraduate handbook which provides
further details about how essays and other written work
should be presented. Always read the course outline and
departmental handbook carefully, and refer to them from
time to time, just to remind yourself of what you should be
doing at any given point in the term. Most of the information
you need will be in these documents, including deadlines for
assessed work and what is expected of you in terms of course
requirements. Hopefully you are interested in the process of
learning and not only focused on what is required of you to
pass the course, but it is still worth knowing how your work
will be assessed or whether there are minimum attendance
requirements in order to successfully complete the course. It is
also useful to familiarise yourself early on with the key aims of
the course, which should be set out in the course outline.

ADDITIONAL SOURCES OF INFORMATION

Find out where the class noticeboard is and keep a regular eye
on it. Any changes to class times and locations will be posted
there or on the course webpage, sometimes at short notice. The
noticeboard and the webpage are also where to look for
workshop groups, exam details and so on. The departmental
office may not be open to student inquiries all day so find out
when the secretary is available. This is where to go if you miss
a workshop and would like to attend another group, if you
want to double-check dates and places for exams, if you
cannot get hold of a particular lecturer, if you change your
address and such like.

All lecturers have office hours – use them; do not suffer in
silence. If you have a problem with any aspect of the course
then go and see the course coordinator about it. Bear in mind
that some academics may prefer face-to-face contact rather
than e-mails and you may receive a better and quicker response in person – e-mails may seem quicker but getting a
reply can be slow, so you are much more likely to get a better

answer to any questions if you speak to the people concerned face to face. However, before asking your particular question, double-check that the answer you require is not in the course outline or departmental handbook. First-year sociology courses can have up to four hundred students on them so lecturers and tutors very much appreciate not being bombarded with queries that are fully explained in the course handouts or at the introductory lectures!

Most universities have student support services that are available for personal problems or learning difficulties as well as offering additional guidance in relation to computer training and study skills such as essay writing, note-taking, time management and exam preparation. If you are experiencing difficulties with any of these, ask your tutor or lecturer whether extra help is available. The sooner you strengthen all of these skills, the more effective, efficient and enjoyable your learning will become.

LIBRARY SKILLS

Get to grips early on with the university library and computers. Make sure you find out how to use them effectively – attend relevant courses that are often offered at the start of the academic year. Using the library properly is more than just looking for books, it also includes searching for journal articles, pamphlets, finding key chapters within books, making use of the photocopy collection and short-term loans (see Chapter 11). Reading lists are often long as this gives students choice and ensures that there are enough available books in the library. This is particularly true of large first-year courses. You will be expected to develop your library and research skills so you can find for yourself the books, chapters and articles that are most useful to your studies. It can also look good if, for your essay, you can find one or two of your own additional sources of relevant literature from academic journals such as those found in recent issues of *Sociology, Sociological Review* or *Sociological Research Online*. Also, searching library resources and chasing up references from bibliographies is all part of the academic 'game' and can actually be rewarding and even good fun – honest! – so give it a go.

It really is best to develop good habits as soon as possible rather than leave it until later years when you have even heavier work-loads and may find yourself losing marks because you do not know how to reference properly or how to present your essay in the correct style for your department. Do not waste marks on something you could easily sort out in your first year. It has to be said that sloppy referencing is rarely looked upon sympathetically once you get beyond your first semester or term at university.

COMPUTING SKILLS

Even if you are a complete technophobe, you should force yourself to find out how to make the most of the available computing facilities. Increasingly, university departments insist that written work be done on a word processor. Some even ask for work to be submitted in an electronic form so that it may be scanned for plagiarism. On a more positive note, a word processor makes editing and revising your work much easier. The computer is also very useful for gathering information from library catalogues and from the internet.

There will almost certainly be courses on computing for new students and they are well worth going to, whether you are computer literate or a complete novice. If you have your own computer at home, it is worth finding out whether your computer is set up in a way that is compatible with the university network. For example, in order to download information from course webpages on the intranet (WebCT) you may need to load 'Adobe' on to your system. Again the university computing support team will help you with such matters. But whatever you do, do not leave it until the day before your essay is due in! The sooner you get yourself some basic computing skills the better. You will probably be given an e-mail address in your first week. So, check your e-mail frequently because this is how your tutors, lecturers or the departmental secretary may get in touch if they need to contact you urgently.

A WORD TO MATURE STUDENTS

If you are a mature student coming to university for the first time, you may have additional pressures to contend with that students straight from school do not have, such as the practicalities of childcare. Your university may provide good-quality, low-cost childcare. If not, it might be worthwhile contacting the children's services department of the local council for a list of registered childcare providers. It is also worth asking the students' union whether there is a mature students' association at your university where you can meet other people who may be in a similar situation to yourself.

You may also have got out of the habit of studying, writing essays and sitting exams and the younger students may seem incredibly self-confident and knowledgeable. There is time during your degree to get into the way of studying and you may well find that your life experience provides you with extra competencies, particularly in relation to time management and communication. Bear in mind that, for lecturers and tutors, teaching mature students can be rewarding because they often have a high level of motivation and ask lots of questions!

FURTHER READING

Bourner, T. and Race, P. (1990), *How to Win as a Part-time Student,* London: Kogan Page. Good advice on managing your time, resources and even your tutors.

McIlroy, D. (2003), *Studying @ University: How to be a Successful Student,* London: Sage. Practical chapters on a range of topics including organisational skills, memory techniques and doing justice to yourself in exams.

Rickards, T. (1992), *How to Win as a Mature Student*, London: Kogan Page. A reassuring discussion of key issues faced by mature students, including acquiring skills and managing time, stress and crises.

Skills4study: http://www.palgrave.com/skills4study/html/index.asp. This website is devoted to resources which can help students study more effectively and includes tips on learning strategies and time management.

10 PLANNING AND TIME MANAGEMENT

Ideally your university experience should be enjoyable as well as challenging. You will find many opportunities to meet new people, join clubs, try new things, as well as being able to access cheap sports facilities and entertainment activities. There should be plenty of time to indulge in these aspects of university life while also studying hard and enjoying sociology! Increasingly (and unfortunately in most cases) many students also have to combine their studies with earning money. However, if you have had to get a job in order to pay your way through university, try to keep your priorities clear. Whilst we sympathise, as we benefited from a grant system, we would urge you not to miss classes in order to go to work. In our experience this will almost certainly lead to anxiety and stress and a decline in your academic performance. We appreciate the difficulties, but try to balance your social life and work with study.

Time management is crucial to a stress-free and rewarding university experience. It is also a key transferable skill valued by employers in a university graduate. Begin at the start of the semester by finding out what is expected of you in terms of all your lectures, workshops and assignments, and write all the classes and deadlines into a diary. Plan your study time outside of lectures and workshops by timetabling it into your diary, allowing time for researching in the library, reading, workshop preparation and writing. Make a list of the key tasks you have to do for each of your courses, and set your own manageable deadlines so you can meet all the coursework requirements throughout the term, leaving plenty of time for exam revision. Build in some extra time in case you are off sick for a few days or for unforeseen circumstances.

Bear in mind that essay deadlines for all your subjects have a nasty habit of falling around the same time, and coming around quicker than you think! This is because lecturers cannot set them too early, as the work will not have been covered, nor too late otherwise students will not benefit from the feedback before the exams. However, pleading that, 'I had three essays to hand in for today. I haven't finished my sociology one. Please can I have an extension?' is unlikely to be a successful strategy. Most lecturers will have a different view of 'deadlines', given that the time between the setting of the essay and the deadline is very generous, perhaps as much as five weeks or more. So, get started as soon as possible after the essay topics are given out. Furthermore, being quick off the mark means that you get to the library before all the books on the reading list disappear.

As well as organising your time throughout the term, you also need to plan your use of time on a daily and weekly basis. As you progressed through school, you will gradually have been given more and more responsibility for your own time management but, between school and university, there is a great chasm. You were expected to get to school at the same time every morning and stay there and work until everybody went home. If you were not at a class, somebody wanted to know where you were. Homework was given in comparatively small, regular amounts and woe betide you if it was not done – we are sure you recognise this scenario.

The strict routine of school, the one that you probably grew to dislike, may now come to be missed. There is a different culture at university and many new students find the transition difficult. First, you may not have a class every day. You may start at nine in the morning, but you might equally not start until the afternoon. You should make sure you establish a good routine. Please do not turn yourself into a robot but the key is to 'stay on top' of your workload. Try not to let it overwhelm you. If you feel this is happening then take steps to sort it out straight away; it will certainly not get any better if you ignore it. Establishing a daily routine can be a good idea, for example, set aside time during the day for reading and build in rewards for sticking to your timetable. Similarly, set yourself weekly tasks and at the end of the week check the extent to which you were able to complete them.

Self-directed learning requires a good deal of motivation and self-discipline. You should recognise that most students (and lecturers for that matter!) often find it difficult to get started, particularly when writing is involved. You need to decide where you are able to study most effectively. Try to find a space where you can think and where you feel comfortable to write. Some students prefer to write ideas on paper first and then type them up, whereas others write directly on to the computer. Find out which enables you to think through your ideas most clearly.

Libraries are usually good places to work, if you can manage to ignore occasional, irritating whisperers. You are less likely to be distracted and go off to do other things than when you are at home such as chatting to flatmates, visiting the fridge or watching your favourite television programme. Going to the library in breaks between classes is also a really good idea, as this is time that can very often be frittered away – do you *really* need to go for all those cups of coffee!

By now you will be aware of the length of time that you can work without a break. You are unlikely to be working effectively if you go for much more than an hour without a rest. You can keep your concentration up for longer if you vary your tasks. So do not set yourself too much reading in one go or you will be unlikely to take it all in. Sit down to study with a realistic target in mind. Reward yourself (with a rest, a chat with friends or reading another chapter of Karl Marx's *Capital*) when you have achieved your goal.

We recognise that with deadlines to meet, sometimes 'doing an all-nighter' may be inevitable. However, if you find that this is becoming a habit you may want to revise your time management. We are not being moralistic here (we were students also!) but we know from our own personal experience, as both former students and lecturers, that the quality of what you produce will probably suffer. Again, it is all a question of sorting out your time management and giving yourself the optimum chance to produce your best work. We often see the consequences of poor work organisation in the dishevelled shape of distressed and anxious students turning up at our doors – try not to let this happen to you.

Finally, effective studying is not only about managing your time and space but also requires you to be well organised. You may feel comfortable about where you are studying and the amount of time you are putting in, but it defeats the purpose if your notes are jumbled up and you cannot find things easily. Develop your own system for organising the material for each of your courses so the lecture notes, workshop and essay preparation, and reading notes are all kept together. Make sure you have a full set of lecture and workshop notes which are up to date and complemented with notes from your reading, which are clearly labelled with full bibliographic details of which books they were from (see Chapter 14 for information on writing a bibliography).

11 READING AND RESOURCES

We cannot stress enough the importance of you building up your reading. Generally you will find that sociological literature can be interesting and engaging and you may well come across a book or writer that can change the way you think. We are clearly biased but we believe you will enjoy much of the reading in sociology as it is about social life and how the world works, or not, as the case may be. Hopefully it should challenge some of your taken-for-granted assumptions and really make you think about the world around you.

Your lecturers will recommend reading to be undertaken along with the lecture course and you really will get far more out of the lectures and the reading if they keep pace with each other. Reading and making notes regularly each week will increase your overall understanding of the course as well as accumulating your knowledge of sociology as a discipline. Sometimes, a lecture course will follow a set textbook quite closely but there will also be additional reading so that you can broaden your knowledge of the subject and assess different points of view.

There will be some texts that are recommended for purchase and, knowing that students can be short of money, lecturers will keep this list to a minimum. It is a good idea to buy one key sociology textbook early on as such general texts are useful for a variety of sociology courses. Good examples are the following:

Bilton, T. et al. (2002) *Introductory Sociology*, 4th edn, Basingstoke: Palgrave Macmillan.
Fulcher, J. and Scott, J. (2003) *Sociology*, 2nd edn, Oxford: Oxford University Press.
Giddens, A. (2001) *Sociology*, 4th edn, London: Polity.

Macionis, J. and Plummer, K. (2002) *Sociology: A Global Introduction*, 2nd edn, Harlow: Pearson.

Marsh, I. et al. (2000) *Sociology: Making Sense of Society*, 2nd edn, London: Prentice Hall.

This list is not exhaustive but we would recommend you only buy one of them as they tend to be quite similar, merely varying a little in relation to style. Each of them covers key chapters on sociological theories, research methods, social divisions (gender, class, race and ethnicity, globalisation), social structures (state, religion, families, education, politics) and social problems (health, crime, poverty, unemployment, deviance). Earlier editions are still relevant but may use slightly more outdated examples. These general sociology texts are useful starting points for both essay and workshop preparation as they are written in an accessible style and the chapters tend to present a clear overview of the main issues and debates. However, a word of warning, do not over-rely on these textbooks, as they do not provide as much depth and complexity as other more specialised literature. You should aim to demonstrate a range of reading rather than overusing one key textbook.

It is also a good idea to obtain a sociological dictionary. These are very useful for clarifying key terms and concepts and to have handy when you are reading and studying; it may well become a 'good companion' to you throughout your degree. There are a number of very good ones on the market, for example, *The Oxford Dictionary of Sociology*, edited by Gordon Marshall (1998).

USING THE LIBRARY

Books that you do not have to buy will be in the library, although bear in mind that there are always more students than books. Right from the start, get to know your library and how it works, especially where the sociology books and journals are kept. The online catalogue will tell you not only where to find books, but also whether they have been borrowed and when they are due back. If a book that you need has been borrowed, you may be able to recall it. Bear in mind there may be more than one place to find books. There are the ordinary open shelves (or stacks) that make up most of the library. In addition, particularly when books are recommended for essays and there is likely to be a huge demand for them, books may be put in a special section of the library where they are available on very short loans. If you have problems, ask a member of the library staff for help.

Plan ahead of time which books you will need and reserve them if they are already in use. We doubt if your lecturers and tutors will listen sympathetically to tales of woe about books not being available. This only tends to happen if you have left your essay preparation until the last moment. It is a good idea to find out which key sociological journals are stocked in your university library or are available online. The main sociological journals in the UK are:

- *Sociology*

- *Sociological Review*

- *Sociological Research Online*

- *Work, Employment and Society*

Often there are many relevant articles in journals which you could use for essay work that are not specifically listed in your course outline, so browse the sociological journals either on the web or in the library to find additional things to read. This is not only a good idea, as you can avoid the rush on books, but browsing journals can also be an enjoyable and productive way to spend some time as you may well come across articles that you will want to read out of interest. When searching for a particular journal article you must look for the name of the journal first (these tend to be organised alphabetically by journal in the section of sociology periodicals of the library and subsequently by date). You can then locate the particular year, volume and issue number of the journal, before finally finding the specific article. For example, you would not be able to find a recent paper by one of the authors under their name as the journal '*Sociology*' would have to be located first:

Punch, S. (2003) 'Childhoods in the Majority World: Miniature Adults or Tribal Children?' *Sociology*, 37(2): 277–95.

(where '37' is the volume number, '(2)' is the issue number, and '277–95' are the page numbers)

Similarly if you are looking for a chapter in a book, you must find the book first and then you will be able to locate the chapter within it. For example:

George, S. (1998) 'How the Other Half Dies', in Marsh, I. (ed.) *Classic and Contemporary Readings in Sociology,* London: Prentice Hall, pp. 266–71.

Use the library catalogue to search for Marsh's book *Classic and Contemporary Readings in Sociology,* and then find the chapter by George. If you search under 'George' you will not find it, unless it is a key chapter which has been made available in a photocopy collection. Bear in mind that if lecturers chose to photocopy particular articles or chapters to make them more readily available, it is likely that it is key material which is worth reading.

Nowadays students can browse the internet to find additional sources of material to use for essays. The web is a great tool but it is also crammed with complete junk and, more problematically, junk that does not always look like junk. So, please be careful when using information from the web and do not over-rely on it. Most university lecturers still prefer students to read books and articles and use these as the basis for their essay work. Use formal or official websites for accessing statistics, recent policy documents or relevant reports (for example, the Economic and Social Data Service (ESDS) website or the *Office of National Statistics*: http://www.statistics.gov.uk). For a list of internet sources, see Winship and McNab (2000). Take care to reference your source by making sure you record the website details and the date you accessed it, and remember that plagiarising from the web is easy to spot because of the availability of 'Google' and other searches.

FINDING RELEVANT MATERIAL

As noted earlier, course reading lists are often long, indicating a broad range of suitable texts. They are designed to offer choice and cater for large numbers of students. You are generally not expected to read everything! Guidance will be given in lectures as to which books are the most useful for particular topics. It can also look impressive if you have managed to find other additional relevant sources which you can refer to in your essay. One way of doing this is when you go to a library shelf to get a particular book, such as old age, look at the other books on those same shelves as they will also be about old age in that area of the library. You may find something else that is useful by browsing along the library shelves or the sociological journals. Remember, you do not just have to stick to the ones on the reading list. Alternatively, the set books or general textbooks might make further reading recommendations or you could do a search on the library online catalogue. Subject searches are not always reliable and sometimes keywords in the title can produce better results. This might produce such a wealth of material that you do not know where to start. So a good guide is the number of times a book or article is cited in other people's bibliographies. This will give you some indication of what is regarded as key reading.

Sometimes reading lists indicate particular chapters in books, but not always, and usually you are not given specific sections to read. This is because you are expected to check out a range of different material and find the relevant information that you need. Remember that lecturers are not going to spoon feed you, and thus will not tell you exactly what page numbers to read in order for you to answer a particular essay question. You should get into the habit of skim reading and looking through a book for the kind of examples you require to back up the arguments you want to make in your essay.

When choosing reading material for essays, allow yourself plenty of time to do background reading and to find key sources. Avoid automatically ploughing through a whole book which may not be directly relevant – a soul-destroying activity! You should think carefully about the essay question first then deconstruct it (see Chapter 14) before making a rough plan of the important points to consider when answering it. Then you will have a good idea of what you are looking for in your reading and of what you might use as examples. When you are browsing, use the contents page or abstract to identify useful and interesting parts and scan read to find the sections you want. Skim through headings and subheadings, read the introduction and conclusion, look at the beginnings and ends of chapters, to see if the book covers what you are searching for. Hence, rather than trying to read everything you can get your hands on, you should be selective about what you choose to read in detail and make notes on. Such a strategic approach to reading will enable you to avoid confusing yourself by reading too much irrelevant material.

NOTE-TAKING

The best academic writers, particularly those who are directing their writing towards first-year students, try very hard to keep their writing clear and easy to read – we hope you give us pass marks! However, it is not always possible to express very complex ideas in very simple language. Furthermore, studying a new subject means learning the terminology of that subject, so some of the reading will be very dry and difficult. The best advice we can give you is that perseverance *will* pay off. Do not put yourself under pressure to 'get' everything first time, try and absorb the gist of the argument or the main points and build up from there, and keep your trusty sociology dictionary to hand for demystifying those scary-looking terms.

The first half of this book will have given you some indication of the type of reading you will have to do and from it you can see that some topics are more readable than others. It is best not to expect much of it to be 'light reading' though. It will demand some 'active reading' on your part, meaning that you will really have to be prepared to work and think along with the text. For this reason, do not under-estimate how long a chapter will take and do not set yourself too big a chunk of reading in one sitting. Occasionally, joint study sessions with other members of your workshop group might be helpful as together you might make more sense of difficult passages – mutual support is always good.

The moment you sit down with a book, make sure you note down all the necessary bibliographical detail, including full title, author, publisher, place of publication, year and page numbers and mark exact quotations in your notes. If you find something you may wish to quote word for word, make sure you get every detail right, including the punctuation. If it contains what looks like an error, put '[sic]' after the error and then everyone will know that you are quoting accurately and the mistake is not yours. Try to use exact quotations sparingly, when you really feel you could not express it in any other way. Quotations should be used as a means to support the points you are raising rather than be left unexplained to speak for themselves. An essay can be augmented and improved by some quotes but too many can be a bit tedious. Lecturers really want to read *your* own work.

Much of your note-taking will consist of paraphrases or summaries of the text but often a passage from a book will spark off your own ideas. Make a note of the passage and write down your responses to it at once, or you will almost certainly forget what they were. Be sure that you make it very clear which notes are exact quotes, which are paraphrases and which are your own thoughts. For example, use different colours of pen or put your ideas in brackets. It is very easy, at a later date, to think an idea is your own when, in fact, you have picked it up in the course of your reading. Strangely, it is even possible to have an original idea and then to convince yourself that you read it somewhere – though this is probably less common! Thus, when you are doing specific reading for an essay and taking notes, put in parentheses comments to yourself about how that point might be relevant for your essay answer.

Notes are an aid to learning, not a substitute for it and you should not just copy down words for future reference. The physical act of writing something down will help to fix it in your mind. If, as you are making your notes, you are already putting arguments and key points into your own words and expressing them in your own way, then you can draw on that for your essay by referencing the text (and page number) rather than over-relying on quotations using other people's words. Once you have finished a chapter or an article, sum-marise the key points of what you have read, so later you can remind yourself at a glance what it was about. This is also useful for revision when learning key points that different authors have made. Clear summaries now will aid revision later on and may serve as memory triggers to spark off remembering greater detail.

If you are using your *own* book or a photocopy, you may want to use a highlighter pen for important sections as well as making notes in the margin which help you identify why it is relevant – doing this to library books is a great 'crime' in our eyes, so please do not do it. Some students seem to use a highlighter as a reading aid and cover what they are reading in a luminous green, pink or yellow. This may make your book instantly recognisable and easy to spot from a long distance but it does defeat the purpose somewhat. Highlighting can make you think analytically by forcing you to be selective and focused, so try to show a bit of highlighting discipline – if nothing else you will save a fortune in pens!

FURTHER READING

Marshall, L. and Rowland, F. (1998), *A Guide to Learning Independently*, Buckingham: Open University Press. A well-written and accessible book which includes how to analyse and research a topic.

Winship, I. and McNab, A. (2000), *The Student's Guide to the Internet 2000–2001*, London: Library Association Publishing. This is very helpful and easy to use but will date very quickly; keep an eye open for updated versions.

12 GETTING THE MOST FROM LECTURES

The main role of lectures is to give you an overview of particular topics, by introducing some of the main debates and key concepts. Lectures are intended to point you in the right direction by highlighting the most important issues as well as serving as a general guide to your reading. Do not rely solely on lectures alone, as they are a starting point but are certainly not the last word on the topic; it is never intended that they should be. In other words, lectures are not a substitute for reading (the reverse is also true). In our experience, students who rely only on lecture notes do poorly and, in terms of sociology, they often just 'don't get it'. Lecturers will always expect to see evidence of your own reading so, when you make a point in your essay, try to find a different example from your reading to illustrate it rather than reproduce the one given in the lecture – take it from us that your lecturer will be bored reading it again, and again. You will receive much better marks for essay and exam work if you are able to draw on a variety of sources and develop those ideas in your own writing style, instead of unimaginatively repeating what the lecturer told you.

As most lecturers provide a lecture programme in the course outline, it is a good idea to take a look at this and get a general picture of where the lectures are heading. Try to think how each specific lecture fits with the course as a whole. In particular, it can be helpful to consider each lecture in the context of the key themes of the course and these are usually highlighted at the introductory lecture and in the course outline. Lectures also tend to offer a focused guideline for coursework and cover exam material so throughout the course you might pick up hints about exam questions.

At the end of a lecture, there may be a short time for

questions. Do not be afraid to ask. If, however, you cannot bring yourself to speak in front of a large audience, have a private word with the lecturer afterwards. Questions can provide useful feedback for lecturers, who need to know whether their lectures are pitched at the right level.

MANAGING DIFFERENT LECTURE STYLES

Remember that the purpose of lectures is for enhancing learning, not for entertainment. You may even find some boring or dull so do not go to lectures expecting to be treated to fifty minutes of stand-up comedy – we would charge an admission fee if that was what was on offer! Shocking as it may be, you may even find that lecturers are not all charismatic and riveting, so, you may have to make a big effort to stop your attention from wandering. Getting the person behind you to poke you with a sharp stick is probably a bit drastic but you should try to listen actively to the main points and concentrate on the central arguments. That way you will improve your concentration and listening skills as well as remember more afterwards. Lecturers have some responsibility to stimulate students' interest and guide them through key issues, but it is up to you to make the most of lectures.

Lecturing styles vary quite a lot: some may use PowerPoint or overheads, some have little or no visual aids at all, others provide handouts either before or after the lecture. These different ways of presenting information are no reflection of the quality of the lecture content. Do not be overly seduced by PowerPoint; focus on what is being said rather than being entranced by multi-coloured slides with words dropping down on parachutes. The brief points from the overheads or Power-Point slides are often made available on a departmental website or may be provided as a handout. If these are accessible on the web before the lecture, you may like to print them off and add notes to them during the lecture. However, we must stress that these are merely aids to make note-taking a bit easier and to help you organise your notes. By themselves they are not enough as you must add the extra detail and explanatory comments. Please do not rely solely on slides and overheads, because if you do your notes will not make sense when you come to revise them. Handouts and PowerPoint slides tend to be an outline of the main points to structure what the lecturer is saying. They are by no means an adequate substitute for attending the lecture itself and getting a full understanding of the topic. Basically, *go* to lectures.

GROUND RULES FOR LECTURES

In lectures you should show consideration for other students and for the lecturer. For example, try not to arrive late as it can be very disruptive and if you have to leave early, warn the lecturer in advance. Similarly, you may not think it matters (we are not sure we did when we were students) if you fall asleep or talk with your friends while the lecturer is speaking, but it is very distracting for both the lecturer and for fellow students. While we are at it, yawning loudly, eating crisps, persistent whispering and swapping little notes (arghh!) is also guaranteed to induce feelings of both anger and paranoia in a lecturer. Some students clearly think they develop powers of invisibility when they enter a lecture theatre but you should be aware that you do not and the aforementioned forms of behaviour are very conspicuous – yes, even those of you who choose to sit at the back. Please note also that the last few minutes of a lecture can provide a very useful summing up of the most important points, and your fellow students and the lecturer will not appreciate it if you start rustling your papers, discussing your evening's entertainment and zipping up your bag because you have decided it is time to be going. So, just try to hang on for another few minutes. Finally, we beseech you, please turn off your mobile phone!

NOTE-TAKING SKILLS

As already mentioned, the information presented on over-heads or PowerPoint slides are like a contents page of a book: it provides the basic structure but not the explanations. As lecturers, we are often surprised at how many students only seem to write down the points that appear on overheads or PowerPoint slides. The rest of the detail, examples and, most importantly, the explanations that lie behind the points then become lost.

However, taking good notes is an acquired skill and is not as easy as it may seem. Initially in lectures many new students find it difficult to be able to listen and pick out the key points, then write them down while listening to the next thing that is being said. You have to try and get used to listening and writing at the same time. In your first year you should aim to develop your note-taking skills as well as your ability to listen actively. Just as lecturing styles vary, so do students' styles of taking notes: some listen more and write little, others take extensive notes. Some students try to write down every word and then get frustrated because they cannot keep up with the pace the lecturer is speaking at. We would recommend that you take comprehensive notes but that you do not try and write everything – believe it or not, not everything a lecturer says is worth writing down! So, you should learn to listen and pick up the key points, and summarise what is most important.

Furthermore, try not to feel intimidated by others around you – do not worry if they are not writing and you are. A minority of first-year students still seem to think that it is 'cool' not to be seen to be working too hard. You may feel self-conscious about writing when they are not, but remember this is your degree and your education; do not let others put you off. In our view, it is certainly better to write too much than too little.

There are several advantages to writing extensive notes rather than just listening. First, you may think you will remember it all but you will not. In fact, the act of writing,

rather than merely listening to someone saying it, means it
is more likely to fix in your mind and be recalled at a later
date. Second, writing helps you to concentrate on what is
being said. It is easy to get distracted while listening for
long periods, which is why note-taking helps focus the
mind. For example, when we are at a seminar or confer-
ence, we nearly always have to take notes otherwise we
soon realise that we are not listening effectively to what the
speaker is saying. So, even if we never need to look at our
notes again and do not need to remember details of their
talk, we still take notes to enable us to concentrate at the
time. Third, good note-taking requires the ability to process
information quickly and capture the main point on paper
while also perhaps sparking off some of your own thoughts
on the topic. If this happens then make sure you write them
down as well. This in turn improves your critical and
analytical thinking. More practically, note-taking can stop
you from nodding off!

Initially you may need to force yourself to get into the
habit of taking notes, otherwise the danger is that you get
used just to listening and will end up thinking that you
cannot listen and take notes at the same time. Remember
that note-making is a skill in itself, so do not worry if you
find it difficult at first. Practise taking notes from the start
of university and you will find that you quickly get skilled
at it.

Developing your own shorthand is a good idea. Some words
will be repeatedly mentioned during your course. For example, when writing notes decide how you want to refer to
common terms such as 'sociology', 'sociological' and 'sociologist' – perhaps 'soc', 'soc-al' and 'soct' Similarly, during a
lecture on a particular topic, certain words will reappear
regularly. For example, in a lecture on the family you may
choose to use the following abbreviations:

ch = children
chood = childhood
ahood = adulthood

yp = young people
hh = household

Put a note to remind you at the top of your lecture notes because, later on, you may forget what the abbreviations mean. You can also use symbols such as:

results in: =
positive: +ve
negative: -ve
therefore: ∴
change: Δ

If you use such terms and symbols often enough, you will become used to their meanings and can use them in all your courses. In addition, you should use bullet points and numbers where possible, particularly to indicate important issues. Rather than write whole sentences, make a note of the main phrases and use a star '*' or a different coloured pen to highlight key terms and important points. This will help with exam revision. The lecturer may tell you the structure of the lecture at the outset, so try to organise your notes accordingly. In particular, if a lecturer repeats a point, it is likely that he or she considers it important for you to write down.

In lectures there is no time for fancy handwriting, just write quickly and legibly, as you can practise your calligraphy later. This will also be a great help in the exam if you can write quickly but clearly – but do not, of course, use your own specialised shorthand and symbols in the exam (except perhaps in your own exam plan).

When taking notes, you should also add your own thoughts, comments and questions. Note down some of your immediate reactions to what the lecturer is saying. What do you agree with? What would you question? What stimulates you to think in fresh directions? Put your response in parentheses, so that you can differentiate it as being your ideas rather than the lecturer's. This can be very helpful when preparing for essays and exams. If there is recommended reading to do, then try to do it as soon as possible after the lecture. Alternatively, doing some reading beforehand can enhance what you get out of the lecture, making it easier to understand and perhaps also easier to remember at a later date.

13 GETTING THE BEST FROM WORKSHOPS

Nearly all sociology courses contain some form of participatory, small-group discussions which take place alongside lectures. Different universities have different cultures and give them various names but, generally, whether they are referred to as tutorials, seminars or workshops, they fulfil the same purpose. Tutorials tend to be smaller with up to about a dozen students with one tutor. Seminars and workshops tend to be larger, with some twenty to twenty-five students per group, but these are often split into smaller groups for discussion during the workshop. For the sake of consistency in this book, we refer to this participatory small group teaching as 'workshops', but your university may prefer to call them tutorials or seminars.

Workshops provide students with an opportunity to raise questions and discuss key sociological debates and concepts. Instead of more passive forms of teaching, such as lectures, workshops require active participation by the students. As we have already mentioned, there is more emphasis on self-directed learning at university and, although this can seem intimidating at first, most students quickly get used to it and enjoy it.

In the first year, you will find that the groups tend to be larger but will probably get progressively smaller throughout your degree. As the format is flexible, different tutors will approach them in different ways. Some treat them as very informal, loosely structured discussions, whereas others use them for slightly more formal, structured debates. Either way, they are usually designed as less informal and more participatory than lectures, and are a key means for students to learn from and with their peers.

The aims of a workshop are to reinforce and clarify any

points that you did not understand in lectures and to explore topics in more depth. Another key purpose of workshops is to stimulate critical thinking in a group context, thus enabling students to develop their own ideas as well as improve their communication. Workshops are designed to enhance and consolidate your understanding of the course, whilst also raising issues that are directly related to your essay writing and preparation for the exams. It is nearly always the case that if students attend and fully participate in all of their workshops, they generally end up with better marks for their essays and exams. You will also be more 'involved' in the course, meet people (possibly future friends) and generally take part in a key aspect of university life.

Often your tutors are not the same people as your lecturers and can be more approachable in what is a less formal setting, so you can take the opportunity to ask questions and check your understanding of key concepts and ideas. Do not be afraid to ask as others probably have similar questions, so you will be doing them a favour as well as yourself. There is usually not much time for questions in lectures, so make the most of workshops to sort out misunderstandings. Tutors tend to have more time to respond to particular questions and to give other relevant examples. If you are stuck with your essay you can possibly speak to your tutor about it. Do not expect any help that would give you an unfair advantage, but your tutor may be able to discuss the topic with you in a very general way. Indeed, the very act of explaining your difficulty can help you to solve the problem yourself.

GROUND RULES IN WORKSHOPS

Workshops are an excellent way of developing a variety of skills particularly in relation to communication: listening, debating and effectively articulating ideas. Tutors will expect you to respect the views of others, not interrupt, not dominate the group and not speak too much or too little. It is unlikely that you will be required to give lengthy presentations in your first year, but you will need to develop your communication skills because in later years you are likely to be required to give a five–fifteen minute talk in workshops. Consequently, use the opportunities to practise speaking out in workshops as early on as possible, no matter how difficult it may seem. The longer you sit in silence the harder it will be to develop those skills which you are expected to foster as part of the university experience. However, if you are more confident you must remember to let other people speak – learning when *not* to talk is an important ability to develop and one that is too often overlooked.

Attendance at workshops is usually compulsory and it is your responsibility to ensure that you sign the attendance sheet. If you know in advance that you cannot attend a workshop because of a hospital appointment or something similar, find out from the departmental secretary whether it is possible to swop to another group for that week. However, do not just turn up without letting someone know beforehand as you need to have your attendance officially noted.

WORKSHOP PREPARATION

Most workshops require advance preparation and the tutor will expect you to have done specific reading or thinking about discussion questions before you turn up. Do not see this as a burden which has to be done as quickly as possible; it is an opportunity for you to structure your reading and learning in relation to the course. Obviously the more you have read, the easier it will be for you to contribute to workshop discussions. Usually for each workshop there will be some key reading for you to do beforehand. If there is a choice, we would strongly advise you to read two of the suggested workshop readings as that way you will get much more out of the workshop.

Most course organisers provide a list of questions or themes to be explored in workshops. These may be indicated in the course outline, or posted on to the web several days before each workshop or given out in the previous workshop. It is a good idea for you to consider these while you are doing your preparatory reading. Furthermore, it is sensible to write notes in relation to the reading you are doing and take these with you to the workshop because you will not remember all the details of what you have read. It also helps to structure these notes around the key workshop questions or topics so that you begin to think how you might go about discussing them in detail during the workshop. You will learn a lot from workshops if you come prepared for them, having spent some time beforehand thinking about key issues and, in particular, having read at least one relevant piece of literature. Hence, the better prepared you are for a workshop, the more you will get out of it.

PARTICIPATION

As well as being expected to have read and prepared for workshops before you turn up, during the workshop itself you are expected to talk and contribute to group discussions. Believe us when we say that participation is key to a successful workshop. So come well prepared, listen to others and offer your own contributions. Workshops can be tricky, and are susceptible to not working very well from both the tutor's and students' point of view. Sometimes a group gels well together, and at other times it just does not seem to work. This can certainly be affected by students' attitudes – the more they make an effort and collaborate, the more likely the workshop is to be successful and useful. Workshops can be great learning experiences if students participate fully, otherwise they can be a grim way to spend an hour or two.

This is not to say that it is not difficult to participate in workshops, but please try to overcome any shyness or lack of confidence by making an effort to take part actively in workshop sessions. You will probably be split into smaller groups, of about five or six students, and it is then that you might find it easier to contribute to discussions. All students are likely to feel that they may have said the wrong thing at some time or another, but if they already knew all the answers, they would not need to be at university in the first place! Trust us, the sooner you get involved the easier and more enjoyable it becomes. In workshops, you are very unlikely to be assessed on what you know (although you should clarify any criteria for assessment with your tutor). If tutors award a mark for workshop performance at all (and not all courses have workshop assessment) it is likely to be based on attendance and participation. Finally, remember to take notes during workshop discussions (even if your colleagues do not) as these will supplement lecture notes and will be very useful when preparing for exam and essay work.

ORAL PRESENTATIONS

Some tutors expect students to give oral presentations in workshops. As already mentioned, it is not very likely that this will happen at the start of your first year. By the time you have to give a talk, you will be more familiar with your subject and friendly with the other members of the workshop group, who are all going to have to go through the same 'torment'. The sooner you practise such presentations, the easier they will become and the quicker you will learn to overcome any nerves.

Your oral presentation will be based on a written paper, produced with all the skills you would use for writing an essay. Many tutors will be quite content if you simply read from your written paper. Your fellow students, on the other hand, may be bored to tears. So the following tips could be useful (see also Robertson and Dearling 2004):

- Be sufficiently well prepared so that your nose is not always buried in your paper

- Mark the important points in your paper with a highlighter pen, so that you can find your way at a glance

- Invite questions and comments and be prepared to deal with them

- Do not be afraid to admit that you do not have all the answers

- With your tutor's permission, make use of any appropriate audio-visual aids (whiteboard, overhead projector, computer screen)

- Provide a handout if you think it would be useful.

14   ESSAY-WRITING SKILLS

An essay is a form of communication and is your attempt to convey to other people your understanding of the topic you are addressing. *Ideally*, your essay should be clear, concise, relevant, logically argued, interesting, well presented and easy to read – now that does not seem too hard, does it? This section gives you some guidelines to help you work towards achieving this ideal. You are unlikely to manage all of this in your first attempt at writing a sociology essay at university level, but it is what you should be aiming for. First year can be seen as a learning opportunity to develop essay writing and exam techniques as these will be different from what has been expected of you at school. In particular, you need to recognise that essay writing is a skill to be cultivated with practice so do not expect to get it all right first time – learning to write well is actually a lifelong task. During your time at university, you will be expected to polish your writing style and adapt to the particular conventions of sociology.

WHY WRITE ESSAYS?

The obvious answer is 'to prove that you have learnt something'. That, however, is not the only, nor the best, answer. If you tackle your essays in the right way, you will find that they are, in fact, a very important part of the learning experience and can provide both a stimulating and enjoyable challenge. It is only when you try to explain things in a totally clear and unambiguous way that you begin to expose little gaps in your understanding. More encouragingly, you may find that, as you arrange your ideas, you make connections that you had not seen before. Remember, writing is a creative process and generally the more effort you put into an essay, the more you will get from it.

Essay writing at university level demands knowledge of the conventions of academic discourse and especially of the way of writing which is appropriate within the academic circle of your particular subject. All academic writing demands attention to detail, not just in the theories you present but also in the manner of presentation and the consistent level of formality that is required. Vocabulary and grammar should be carefully checked to eliminate misunderstandings and sources of information have to be cited and a bibliography provided.

Many university departments insist on the use of word processors for essays and you should take advantage of any computing courses for new students. Furthermore, in your first year at university there are likely to be workshops and/or lectures on essay skills and we would strongly advise you to attend as they will stand you in good stead throughout your degrees. In such sessions you will be given advice on how to structure your essays, how to build arguments and adopt the appropriate essay style and so on. It is also a good idea to acquaint yourself with the criteria used for marking your essays as well as your university's grading scheme, both of which are likely to be in an undergraduate departmental handbook (see section on 'Learning from Feedback' below).

Before you start preparing for your essay, find out about the submission requirements: word limit, the formatting style of your department, the deadline and rules about lateness. It is always worth knowing the extent to which assessed essay work counts to your overall grade for each course. Most importantly, keep to the required deadline and do not perceive it as something that is potentially flexible. Remember that the deadline is the last time to hand your essay in by, but if you cannot manage to hand it in on that date or time, then hand it in the day before or even several days before! Many universities are strict about not granting extensions for essays unless students have written proof of a valid reason why they were unable to hand their work in on time. This may seem a bit harsh, but if you are late for a train it does not wait for you, and in the 'real' world of work, most deadlines cannot be extended under any circumstances.

Some departments provide a set essay question and there is no scope for choice. If you have an opportunity to choose from several questions, make sure you choose a topic that interests you as this will increase your motivation for reading in that area. In a sociology essay you are often required to question taken-for-granted assumptions and to use evidence to support your arguments. Your essay should incorporate some theoretical element by using different aspects of sociological theories to build your explanations (see Chapter 4). A sociology essay will generally consist of the following:

- **Title page:** the essay question written out in full (do not adapt it); your student ID (either your name or registration number depending on whether essays are marked anonymously or not), title of the course, your tutor's name and the word count.

- **Introduction:** the introduction tells the reader what the essay is about by outlining your interpretation of the question. It also sets out the structure you have adopted for the essay.

- **Main section:** this section develops the key points of the argument in a logical progression. It uses evidence from research studies (empirical examples) and theoretical arguments to support these points.

- **Conclusion:** the conclusion sums up your main ideas and reassesses the arguments in order to make a final statement which directly answers the essay question.

- **References:** this is a list of the full bibliographic details of the publications you referred to in the text of your essay.

Rather than being a single big task, writing is a process involving a variety of tasks:

Planning: researching information and constructing a plan
Structure: organising relevant material in a logical manner
Content: presenting a reasoned argument which is both critical and analytical
Style: writing clearly and concisely in your own words
Referencing: using appropriate academic conventions
Proof-reading: revising the final draft and preparing for submission
Learning from feedback: reflecting on ways to improve your next essay.

The rest of this section concentrates on guiding students through each of these seven tasks.

PLANNING

One of the keys to successful essay writing is careful planning and preparation. You need to plan in advance how best to use your time effectively so you have enough time to read, make notes, structure an outline of your essay, write a first draft, edit it and do a final version. Remember that there will be pressure on books the week before an essay deadline so it is a good idea to do at least some of your reading and preparation early.

Interpreting essay questions

In order to plan your essay answer, you should be clear about exactly what the question is asking you to do, so spend time on making sure you fully understand the question. Not answering the essay question is an all too common way students lose marks, so try to learn to interpret questions by scrutinising the wording of the question. There are certain recognisable types: *Discuss* ..., *Compare and contrast* ..., *Critically examine* ..., *Analyse* ..., *Evaluate* ... Make sure you undertake the activity asked for. Does the question have two parts to it, requiring you to tackle more than one aspect of a particular issue? Does it specifically ask you to provide particular examples or draw on specific case studies to illustrate your answer?

Sociology essays will not merely require you to describe an issue, but will nearly always expect you to try to *explain* it. Bear in mind that most topics which sociologists address are complex and cannot be explained in a simplistic manner. Try to recognise the contested nature of sociology, so that your answer captures some of the complexities of the social world. It is also worth noting that there are often several different ways of tackling an essay question and that all students' essays on the same topic will end up being different, not least because they will have drawn on different resources. This is a point to bear in mind when you are comparing your essay to those of other students. Thus, during the planning stages you may need to choose which angle to approach the question from and which kind of examples you will focus on. Usually you have to make a decision about breadth or depth: whether you draw on a wide range of examples or opt to focus on one or two key case studies to illustrate your arguments.

Everything you write should be relevant to the question: irrelevancies will not gain marks and they will even lose you marks by taking up space that should have been used on answering the question. Word limits on essays are based on the assumption that every word is necessary and to the point. If you are in any doubt what an essay question means, ask for clarification.

Planning and organisation

As mentioned, one of the most important aspects to writing a good essay is to make sure you plan it well. It should probably take you longer to read and write notes, write a plan and prepare for your essay than actually writing it. During the planning stages ask yourself the following questions (adapted from Marshall and Rowland 1998: 85–7):

1 *What does the question mean?*
- examine the wording of the question: what are you expected to cover, what is the purpose of that particular question?

- what are the key terms or concepts, and which will need to be clearly defined? (Use a general sociological textbook for a glossary of terms or a dictionary of sociology)

- how will you focus on the question: which issues will you concentrate on and which theories and examples will you draw on?

2 *What knowledge do you have of this topic?*
- brainstorm your initial thoughts

- what are the most important aspects of answering the question? Look at the information you already have from lecture notes and workshop discussions, then complement with wider reading

3 *What is your position in relation to the question?*
- do you agree or not, or to some extent?

- how would you argue this question and what are your reasons?

4 *What are the main points?*
- write a list of relevant points and see whether they can be grouped together as larger issues so that you end up with approximately four–six main points

5 *How might the main points link together?*
- work out a logical way to structure your arguments: which point should come first and how can it link into the next point and so on?

6 *What evidence will you use?*
- develop and expand each point with relevant examples

- ensure that you reference all your sources of information

Write a detailed outline of your essay and make sure you are confident that your main points answer the question and that you know where your essay is going before you start writing it. Much of the information you need will have been covered in lectures and reinforced in workshops. A good essay, however, shows signs of additional reading which has obviously been well understood and used appropriately. Think how the notes from your reading will fit into your essay plan and where you may use examples from your reading to back up your points. A very good essay will also demonstrate some creativity in answering the question, perhaps by tackling it from an original angle.

STRUCTURE

Students are usually surprised at how much importance markers attach to the structure of essays. Anybody can regurgitate descriptive information but this is not what essay writing is about. Markers are looking for the ability to manipulate information in an analytical way and to provide explanations. Generally, in a sociology essay, you are expected to think critically and construct some kind of argument. In this context, argument does not necessarily mean anything confrontational, it simply means that your essay should have a clear thread running through it.

Sometimes the wording of an essay title indicates a structure: 'Discuss the advantages and disadvantages of using interviews in qualitative research.' This rather suggests an introduction which defines interviewing and qualitative research, and goes on to outline which methodological issues will be addressed and why. This would be followed by a discussion of the relative pros and cons of each issue. The closing paragraph would sum up the main points and comment on the appropriateness of interviewing for conducting qualitative research. It could perhaps also indicate whether there are more advantages or disadvantages to using this research method. The structure of the main section would be likely either to discuss the advantages and then the disadvantages, or may take each methodological issue in turn and comment on its relative benefits and limitations.

If no obvious structure suggests itself, experiment with different ways of writing an essay plan and put the core idea down on the middle of a bit of paper and let other ideas branch off. These secondary ideas might generate their own branches, which might each form a section or paragraph of your argument. Do not worry if the same idea crops up in two places but ask yourself if that produces a possible link between sections. You might prefer a more linear plan, like a flow chart, or you might try grouping related information, listing pros and cons, identifying major themes and so on. If no plan emerges, do not despair as sometimes the act of writing brings the necessary insights. To generate some ideas one trick worth trying is to write as fast as you can for at least three minutes without stopping to think or lifting your pen. It does not matter if you write nonsense – just get something relating to the essay topic on paper to expand, re-order and improve.

Once you have decided on the issues you will cover, try and group them together as four to six key ideas that your essay will address. Each of these major points may have two or three subpoints encompassed within them, which you will develop across one to three paragraphs before moving on to the next main point. Consider how each of your four to six key ideas best slot together: which point should you make first and which point does it logically lead into? Then ask yourself where it should continue from there and what is most appropriate for the final point. Ideally, each point should add to the one before, to build up your argument. More importantly, each point should contribute directly to answering the question that has been set. Your overall aim is to achieve a logical organisation to your essay so that it has some kind of clear structure.

Subheadings can be useful when organising and planning

your work, but do not leave them in as your essay should flow without needing subheadings to direct the reader. To enhance the clarity of your essay's structure, use pointers in the essay which signpost what you have already argued and where the essay is heading next. For example: 'Thus we have seen that . . .' or 'Now it is appropriate to turn to the question of . . .' You should guide the reader through your essay to make it really easy for him or her to read and know where it is going. Having a clear structure to your essay will also help you to avoid making irrelevant points or digressing. The old adage for a basic essay structure has much to commend it:

- Say what you are going to say

- Say it

- Say that you have said it

Your essays should always have the basic structure of a beginning, middle and end. It is worth learning early on what makes a good introduction and conclusion as these should always frame the main body of ideas in your essays (see the Appendix for specific examples of good and bad ones).

The introduction

An introduction leads the reader into your essay as opposed to a conclusion which sums it up as a whole. You have to decide how you are going to interpret the question and how you are going to go about answering it. The purpose of the introduction is to establish this for the reader, making it clear how you will focus the essay, what you are going to cover, how you define key terms and how your essay will proceed. Thus, the introduction does three things: first, it aims to arouse the reader's interest; second, it shows that you have a good understanding of the question; and third, it establishes the structure of your essay.

Use your introduction to ensure that the structure of your essay is really clear for the reader: say what you will do and in what order. It will help your reader to understand your essay if you give an overview of where you are heading. You could state your objectives or list the main issues you intend to deal with (in the order that they appear in your essay) or say briefly what you intend to explain or discuss. Present a clear guide as to where the essay is going. For example: 'First, the essay begins by looking at . . . Second, it examines . . . Subsequently, the essay discusses . . . Finally, it ends by showing that . . .' Ensure that the structure of the essay is clear, so that the reader does not lose the thread of your argument.

It is often a good idea to write the introduction last, because by then you will know exactly what your essay is about. However, some students may find that writing the introduction early on helps to direct them and keep them to the point. If that is the case for you, at least make sure you edit it at the end and check that it really sets out what you ended up doing. Bear in mind that not all essay titles require the same style of introduction so you will need to tailor it to the particular requirements of each question. For example, some essay titles call out for certain terms to be defined, or for a bit of background information to be given, or for reasons for focusing the essay in a particular way. Sometimes you may need to show an awareness that the essay could be tackled in many ways, but you explain why you are going to concentrate on a specific aspect in depth. Usually an introduction is just one paragraph and it should not be more than two.

The main section

In the main body of your essay you should aim to address the question directly, backing up your arguments with evidence from your reading while doing what you said you would do in the introduction. There are no hard and fast rules on how to go about answering an essay question, and there are many different ways of doing it. Having said that, your essay is likely to consist of approximately four to six substantial points which together build an argument for answering the question. Thus you make each point, develop and expand it, and back it up with an example from relevant literature. You then link that point into the next point. Do that four or five times, and you have your main section. The important thing is that the body of your essay focuses on your argument and you use illustrations from your reading to justify the points you are making rather than merely structuring the main section around a list of examples.

The conclusion

The final paragraph should not introduce any new material or any new ideas but should round off your essay. A conclusion should do two key things: summarise the main arguments of your essay and conclude with a final comment which relates to the essay question. Thus, it should pull everything together and make a final evaluation of the material you have used. For example, in relation to a question about how age is used to organise societies, a final concluding statement might be: 'Therefore this essay has argued that age can be used in a variety of ways to structure societies but it can be seen that British society is particularly ageist.' Certainly you will not go far wrong if your closing paragraph briefly restates the question and says how you have answered it. If you cannot show in your final paragraph that you have answered the question, perhaps you should ask yourself if you really have done so. Nevertheless, take care not to make broad sweeping statements such as 'I have proven that . . .' or 'My research has definitely shown that . . .' It is usually more appropriate to state your claims within the limits of your essay. For example: 'The evidence presented here seems to suggest that . . .' or 'In this essay it has been argued that . . .' Do not leave the reader with an ambiguous conclusion and remember that is the last thing they read, so take time to finish your essay well.

CONTENT

Developing arguments

Think about how you will develop your arguments through the essay in order to answer the question. Which sociological theories are relevant to use? What sociological concepts might be appropriate (for example, power, inequality, ideology, identity)? What arguments are put forward by different sociologists in the literature? Decide what your central points are, then consider how you might illustrate them by using examples to reinforce your argument.

The content of your essay should demonstrate your ability to reason and argue. Try to present balanced arguments, rather than focusing on just one issue, and show awareness of any contradictions or tensions. Remember that you are seeking sociological explanations which require you to question taken-for-granted assumptions and this may mean recognising that the nature of the social world is often debated from different viewpoints. So, aim to show that you are thinking critically.

Importantly, try to keep each point separate even though there may be some overlaps with interconnecting issues. Avoid jumping from one point to another and then back again. Planning is the key to not ending up being too repetitive or having too many ideas jumbled up together: be clear what each point is and how they link together. If you have to keep saying, 'as I said earlier', you may want to rethink your essay structure.

Providing evidence

Consider how you will incorporate what you have read into your own essay writing. Not only should you reference all the sources of the points you make, but you will also need to substantiate your arguments with empirical evidence. Use examples of research which you have gathered during your reading and make sure there is a clear link between the example you are using and the argument you are making. On the one hand, try not to let the examples stand by themselves but explain why you are using them and what they illustrate. On the other hand, do not go into too much detail with the example by wasting words on describing the study. Assume the reader is familiar with the case study you are referring to (or can look it up from your reference) and that way you will be able to draw on a range of different reading material rather than over-rely on just one or two pieces you have read. Think about how to use the material in an interesting and appropriate way.

Answering the question

Make sure that everything you say is relevant, if necessary, point out why it is relevant. A common error is that students merely write everything they know on the topic instead of ensuring that what they write is clearly relevant to answering the specific essay question. Every now and then it is a good idea to make a direct link between what you are saying and what the essay question asked you to do. Remind the reader, at the start or end of paragraphs, how the point addresses a particular part of the essay question. In order to do this effectively, it can be a good idea sometimes to use keywords from the question to demonstrate why your points are relevant. It is up to you to make a link between what you read and how you put your arguments together in order to answer the essay question. Remember that you will not find a book that has the answer to the essay question in it and ultimately it is your responsibility to construct your answer by drawing on a variety of reading materials.

Beware of trying to make things relevant when they are not just because you read something on it! If you find that the chapter you read was not that useful for answering this question, then keep your notes for the exam or consider it as expanding your knowledge. Similarly, if you feel your reading and preparation means that you cannot answer one part of the question, try to fill that gap by doing some further reading. Finally, remember that your essay may be extremely interesting and brilliantly written, but if it is not directly related to the question that is being asked, you will lose marks.

Getting started

If you are having difficulty getting started, remember that you do not have to start at the beginning. Some of the ideas that you have jotted down while reading and note-taking can be written out to form a series of nuclei around which you can build up your text. Then you can fit them into your planned structure and, if the words still will not come, try talking. Explain what you are trying to write to your flatmate, your cat or your bathroom wall, and write down exactly what you said.

When you have plenty of ideas, just concentrate on getting them all down. Whether you use a word processor or pen and paper, just enjoy the experience. Worry about spelling, grammar and the exact words later. An essay which overflows with ideas and has to be refined is better than one that has to be padded out. Stay flexible as what you write may give you new inspiration. You may find connections you had not noticed before and you may need to revise your essay plan a bit. It is very easy to move chunks of text around on your word processor, so experimenting with structure is not a problem. However, when you move text around, make sure that any seams do not show by reading it over to check that the section you have moved links into its new surroundings.

STYLE

Clarity

So far we have discussed the structure and content of your essay, and now we turn our attention to style, which includes both the presentation and clarity of your material. Do not underestimate how important style is by spending all your time worrying about content. You are expected to be able to write clearly and to know basic grammar, punctuation and spelling. Making sure your essay is well presented will put your assessor in a good frame of mind when he or she starts to read your work – never a bad idea!

At university, you will be assessed primarily on what you write and that is inseparable from *how* you write. It does not matter how much you know if you cannot get that knowledge down on paper in a way that makes sense to the reader. You need to check that individual sentences and paragraphs are clear and concise while also ensuring that the essay makes sense as a whole. Use your words wisely: try not to waffle or say the same things in different ways as too much repetition is a waste of your word limit.

Try not to be vague, for example, when you use a pronoun, can you identify the exact word or phrase it replaces? *This*, *these*, *that* and *those* are real danger words. After a long ramble, students often write, 'This means . . .' when it is not at all clear what 'this' was. Once you feel confident that you understand your material, try to articulate it to the reader as effectively as possible. You cannot assume that, just because the reader is an expert in the subject, he or she will know what you are trying to say.

Effective communication is what makes good writers stand out. When you are writing essays, it is very easy to fall into the trap of thinking that this is between you and the page, forgetting that a real person is going to have to read it and perhaps even enjoy it. If you do not fully understand what you are writing about, this will be extremely obvious to the person marking it. Remember that writing simply and getting your ideas across in a clear manner is far more important than using fancy phrases that run the risk of not making sense.

Sentences

The important thing about sentences is to keep the words in the right order. Each sentence should have a verb – it sounds obvious but many students seem to forget this at times. If you are building complex relationships, your sentence might have to be long, but long sentences can be confusing. Hence, if you are trying to express a complex idea, it is often a good idea to split it up into shorter sentences. Also, try to make sure your sentences link to one another, so that one sentence follows on from the one before and that it relates to the sentence that follows.

Paragraphs

Try not to put too many ideas or unconnected points into one paragraph but introduce a new theme or aspect of your argument in each new paragraph. Avoid writing in really long rambling paragraphs or ones that are too short as they can make your essay seem disjointed. A paragraph should have at least three sentences; most will have about six or seven, but certainly it should not go on for a page. In the best writing, one paragraph naturally and necessarily flows on to the next. Between paragraphs, take time to reflect by asking yourself: what did I establish in the last paragraph and how does my next paragraph relate to it? In case the relationship is not immediately clear, it is useful to have a few strategies ready to enable you to link paragraphs to each other. For example, it might be helpful to use connecting words and phrases such as the following:

Enumerative: *First . . . Second . . . Finally . . .*

Additive: *Another example . . . Furthermore . . . Moreover . . . In addition . . .*

Contrastive: *By contrast . . . On the one hand . . . On the other hand . . . Alternatively . . .*

Conclusive: *Consequently . . . Therefore . . . As a result . . . Hence . . . Thus*

When you are reading, make a note of any links which you think are effective and which you would feel comfortable using. Beware, however, of overusing any of these links as they can easily become intrusive and irritating. Watch your writing very carefully for links that are becoming too much of a habit, for example, people often pepper their work with the words 'however' and 'thus'.

Writing style

Do not rely on a computer grammar check because they are not sophisticated enough. If you know your grammar or punctuation are weak then consult study guides that will be available in your library. Always write out full versions of words rather than using apostrophes for shortened words, for example: *there's = there is, they're = they are, didn't = did not.* Similarly, avoid writing in a chatty style or informal tone by not using colloquial expressions and slang terms.

Departments, and even individual lecturers, vary in their acceptance of the use of *I* in academic writing. Generally it is only acceptable to use *I* in the concluding paragraph when you are making it clear where you stand in relation to the essay question on the basis of the arguments you have put forward. In the main body of your essay it is usually best to avoid the use of *I* and writing in the first person. Rather you should write in the third person, such as: *This essay argues that . . .* or use a passive construction, such as: *It can be argued that . . .* This will enable you to keep to a more formal style of writing and to avoid slipping into more personal anecdotes.

Spelling mistakes create a bad impression especially when you make mistakes with technical terms specific to your subject. Keep a good dictionary close to hand and also watch for words that are spelt right but have the wrong meaning in that context, such as their/there or too/two. Many spelling or grammatical mistakes can be an indication that you have rushed your essay and have not taken the time to read it through carefully before handing it in.

Use punctuation to enhance the clarity of your writing, but remember that too much punctuation can get in the way of fluent reading. Should you put a piece of punctuation in the wrong place, it is obvious that you do not know what you are doing, whereas if you leave a piece of punctuation out it looks like a little typing error. Exclamation marks should be avoided (unlike the style adopted in this book!) as they have very little place in academic discourse.

Presentation

Nowadays most departments expect you to word process your essay. The advantage of using a computer is that you can do several drafts. You can read it through and easily make adjustments. You can change the order of your main ideas, you can add extra points and take out repetition or irrelevant sections. This form of editing your essay on the computer is highly recommended as it greatly improves the final version that you hand in.

A departmental style sheet, telling you how to set your work out, is usually available to help you prepare your essay for submission. Check the course or departmental handbook for such information. If not, here are a few suggestions:

1. Make sure your type face is big enough: 12 pt is easy on the eye and generally acceptable.
2. A page with plenty of white space is more attractive than a black, solid block of text so be sure to use big margins, so that the marker can write helpful comments, and only type on one side of the paper. For the same reason it is best to avoid single spacing as this will limit the space that markers have for making comments and it makes text tough to read.
3. If you are quoting more than three lines you should indent the quotation:

> Moreover, you need to choose the right words in
> order that you may make your meaning clear not only
> to your reader but also to yourself. The first requisite
> for any writer is to know just what meaning he wants
> to convey, and it is only by clothing his thoughts in
> words that he can think at all. (Gowers 1987: 3)

Note that, when indentation is used for a quotation, there are
no quotation marks.

4. Imaginative use of fonts may help to make a point but,
   for the main body of your text, avoid weird and
   wonderful fonts.
5. Usually in essays you will not need to use footnotes or
   endnotes as these tend to be used in longer dissertation work. Your departmental style sheet may give a
   ruling on this. If not, and you do wish to use them, try
   to do whatever helps the reader. It is an irritation
   constantly having to flick to the end of a text. On the
   other hand, too many footnotes on a page can make
   for a very ugly appearance. For a few short notes
   which are important to the understanding of the text,
   the foot of the page is best. If they are copious and
   more for form than necessity, tuck them away at the
   end.

REFERENCING

Referencing can seem quite daunting as you probably have not
had to do it before, so spend time now getting to grips with
how to do it properly because you will have to do it throughout your university life. Students often ask how many references they should include in their essay and there is no set
answer to this. It depends on how much reading you have
done and on how your essay is structured. Nevertheless, as a
rough guide, sociology lecturers would probably be surprised
to see a first-year essay with less than four, or more than

twelve, chapters, books or articles in the bibliography. For example, if you made four main points in your essay you would reference the source of each of these, plus the examples you use to back them up, thereby totalling eight texts. Bear in mind that you might refer to a key book several times throughout your essay but try to avoid using the same text three or four times in one paragraph.

Instead of over-relying on just one or two introductory texts, try to use a variety of reading materials. Certainly the better essays tend to draw on a range of different texts, arguments and examples. Students are more likely to get a better grade if they put in more preparation time by doing more reading. However, beware of just listing examples and not making them relevant to the essay title. Be selective and accept that you will not be able to include everything you have read. Choose the most appropriate examples to illustrate your point. As a rough guide, a marker would tend to expect to see at least one or two different references per paragraph. If you look at a page of your essay and there are no references at all, then you need to think carefully about the source of your ideas.

The purpose of references and bibliographies is to enable your readers to find for themselves the material to which you have referred. They may want to check your accuracy or, more positively, they may be stimulated by your writing to go and find out more. Whenever you are picking up another author's idea, even if you are not using the exact words, it is usual to use the author's surname, the date of publication and the page number in parentheses (Wiseman 1997: 32) after the citation or, if the author's name is part of your text, just bracket the date and the page number: Wiseman (1997: 32) is a fictitious example. If you are making a general point that is the key theme of a book or chapter, you do not need to specify the page number. If an author has more than one publication of the same date, these are designated 1997a and 1997b.

If you are using quotations you must add the page number and use quotation marks. For example: 'The relationship between capitalism and patriarchy is a dynamic and changing

one and it impacts differently on different groups of women'
(Abbott 2000: 83). Use exact quotations sparingly, mainly
when you think the phrase sums up an idea much better than
you could express it yourself. Quotations should not be too
long nor left to speak for themselves but should be explained
and blended into your text. It can be quite effective to use one
in your introduction or conclusion if it encapsulates the central
argument of your essay. Once again, there are no fixed rules,
but your assessor is unlikely to approve of more than one
quotation per paragraph, and probably not more than four or
five in total.

Most of the time you will be paraphrasing and summarising
ideas from the literature and adding the reference which shows
the source of that information. In this way you demonstrate that
you fully understand the points you are making rather than
merely relying on someone else's words. For example, the following examples have been paraphrased from Bauman and May:

- Our self-identity has a social basis, and the distinction
  between 'us' and 'them' helps us to define who we are
  (Bauman and May 2001: 30).

- According to Bauman and May (2001: 30), our self-identity
  has a social basis, and they argue that the distinction
  between 'us' and 'them' helps us to define who we are.

Note above the two different ways of referencing either in
parentheses after your own words or directly incorporating
the reference to the authors into your sentence. Proper referencing is essential if you are not to be accused of plagiarism,
which is the stealing of other people's ideas or writings.

Plagiarism, whether intentional or unintentional, is a form
of cheating which universities are very concerned about. They
are also becoming increasingly vigilant to ensure that students
do not copy work from other students, from published sources
or from the internet. Of course in any essay you will present
and discuss other people's ideas, opinions and theories, but
you always need to say where you found them and you must

be very careful not to claim them as your own original thoughts.

Writing a bibliography

Bibliographies can be a real chore, but the task can be made a lot easier if you note all the necessary information right from the very beginning of your research. It is soul-destroying chasing round the library looking for things like page numbers and place of publication when the rest of the job is done. The perfectionist will ensure that the latest editions of books are consulted wherever possible, but, if you cannot get hold of the most recent edition, list the one that you actually referred to in your bibliography.

The exact formats for bibliographies vary greatly and attention should be paid to where full stops, commas and colons are used. The key is to be consistent with your use of punctuation. Use the recommended style for your department and keep to the same format throughout. It is not necessary to separate out books, chapters and journals as the bibliography is usually one list in alphabetical order (by the author's surname). If there is no set format in your department, the following are possible options.

Book: Author, A. N. (1995) *Book Title in Italics*, Place: Publisher.
Bauman, Z. and May, T. (2001) *Thinking Sociologically*, Oxford: Blackwell Publishers.

Chapter in a book: Author, A. N. (1996a) 'An Essay in a Book', in S. Cribble (ed.) *Book Title*, Place: Publisher.
Abbott, P. (2000) 'Gender', in G. Payne (ed.) *Social Divisions*, London: Macmillan.

Journal article: Author, A. N. (1996b) 'Article Title', *Italicised Journal Name*, 10 (3): 1–55.
Schildkrout, E. (2002) 'Age and Gender in Hausa Society: Socio-economic Roles of Children in Urban Kano', *Childhood*, 9 (3): 344–68.

Internet sources: If you are referring to a website, you must make sure that you give enough information so that a reader could access the same site. Give the date in case the site has been updated since you used it. For example:

Globalisation Guide (2002) *Australian Apec Study Centre*, http://www.globalisation-guide.org/03.html, updated 2002, accessed September 2002.

Lecture notes: You may wish to make a point in your essay that you got from a lecture, but do not over-rely on this. It is not very impressive if you base most of your essay just on lecture notes and you will end up with a poor grade. However, if there is a particular argument which was raised in the lecture but you have been unable to find a similar point in your wider reading, then you should reference the lecturer and lecture notes in much the same way as you cite other materials:

In your essay:

The relationship between class and inequality is complex (McIntosh 2005).

In the bibliography:

McIntosh, I. (2005) *Lecture Notes: Class and Inequality*, Stirling: Stirling University.

PROOF-READING

Do not rush the final stages of essay writing as you do not want to lose marks because of simple errors that could easily have been corrected. No matter how saturated you are with your essay, force yourself to read it through carefully at least once before handing it in.

Stage one: It is very difficult to proof-read your own work and the more of a distance you can put between writing and re-reading the better. If possible leave your essay for at least a day and come back to it when you have a clear head. If not, you read what you *think* is there rather than what is actually on the paper.

Stage two: Read for general sense and good communication. It can be worthwhile reading your work out loud to check whether the essay really says what you want it to say. Are there any bits that are unclear or sound rather pompous? At this stage, do not stop to correct things or you will lose the big picture so just make a mark in the margin. Have you got the balance right, spending most time on the most important points? Are your arguments backed up with examples and references? Is it coherent and overall does it hang well together? Watch out for repetition because sometimes, after previous cutting and pasting, the same sentences can appear twice. Once you have read the essay right through, wrestle with the awkward sentences, and be careful that any edits you make do not introduce new errors.

Stage three: Do the mechanical bits in turn. Use the spellchecker but do your own check for things that it will miss like *it's/its*, *where/were*. A very common kind of mistake is to mistype the little words, *on* instead of *of* for example. Is your punctuation helpful? Double-check names and dates, physically look up everything that you have cross-referenced. When checking your grammar, common errors to look out for include verbs changing tense and pronouns drifting between one and you, sentences without verbs, run-on sentences where there should be a full stop in the middle, singular verbs with plural subjects and singular subjects with plural verbs. Also make sure all pages are numbered and are in the right order.

Stage four: Give it to someone else to read, not necessarily a specialist in your subject. Ask that person to make sure he or she can completely understand every sentence. In this way, your own understanding will be tested. Offer to do the same for your colleague as you can learn a lot about your own writing from helping to make other people's writing clearer.

LEARNING FROM FEEDBACK

The grade you achieve for your essay might seem like the most important feedback you can get, but take careful note of the comments from the marker. You should get written feedback on an assessment sheet as well as comments noted on the actual essay. If you have the opportunity to collect your work from the person who marked it, then listen to what he or she says about how you could improve your grade in the future. You may be disappointed if you got a bad grade, or very happy because you did better than you thought, but still try to take advantage of hearing any feedback you are given rather than just concentrating on your grade. For example, your essay may have been good on content but poor on style, you may be referencing incorrectly, or not structuring your essay appropriately. Pay close attention to all the feedback you get and if you have any queries about how you may improve certain aspects of your writing, then go and see your tutor.

Feedback on an assessment sheet is likely to be split into different aspects of essay writing, such as content, structure, focus, expression and presentation. Reflect on the comments that you are given in relation to each technique and try to find out how to improve your essay-writing skills. Try to learn from your mistakes and aim to improve your technique each time you write an essay. You will gradually develop your own writing style but do not leave this learning process until the second or third year of your degree. Find out where you are going wrong now so that you can start to work on any weaknesses as soon as possible.

The following are common problems with students' essay-writing technique:

- **Failure to understand the question:** to avoid this, scrutinise the question (see section on 'Planning' above) and if you are unsure, check with your tutor that your understanding of the question is appropriate. Make sure you know what the key terms in the essay question are, and remember to explain them in your introduction rather than just jumping straight in.

- **Descriptive not analytical:** lower grades tend to be given if the essay is just descriptive: listing information without being selective or developing an argument. Higher grades are given for work that demonstrates analytical and critical thinking, and that uses sociological concepts which are relevant to the question asked.

- **Lack of focus or structure:** try not to wander off the point you are making but to keep tightly focused on the arguments you planned to make. In the main part of the essay, do what you said you would do in the introduction without going off at tangents. Plan your essay well, and work out a clear structure before you start, then stick to it.

- **Irrelevance:** make sure that each point you raise is clearly relevant to answering the question rather than just interesting, additional information that is not directly relevant. Some essays just ramble on and it is unclear as to how they are addressing the question that has been set. Think about the essay title before you do your reading so that you can focus your reading and know what kinds of material you are looking for.

Criteria for marking essays

The course outline or departmental handbook should tell you what the marks really mean in terms of whether you have just passed, or passed well, or passed outstandingly. Go by what the handbook says rather than by comparing yourself with other students. You may be surprised to discover that, at least in the first year of a university course in sociology, students are not expected to be particularly innovative. There is a lot of groundwork to be learned before you are ready to produce original work. Occasionally, students are worried because they feel they are not writing anything new but merely reproducing what they have heard in lectures and read in books and articles. Essay writing in sociology is more than just mindless copying out of facts. What the marker is looking for is the ability to handle all the information, to select the bits that answer the question and to put them together in a meaningful way. If you can do all that, you are demonstrating an understanding of the subject and an ability to think analytically and critically. Where you can use creativity and originality is in your selection of examples to illustrate the points you are making.

It is useful if you know in advance exactly how your essay will be assessed, so that you realise that a variety of factors produce a competent essay. It is certainly not all about content and understanding the question but is also about style and writing technique. A range of criteria are taken into account when deciding on your final grade. Thus, markers are not only concerned with *what* you write but *how* you write it. They look for well-rounded and balanced work that demonstrates a variety of skills that are involved in the process of crafting an essay answer.

Essays are the most demanding pieces of writing that you will be asked to do in first year. In later years, you may be asked to do a much longer dissertation and you may even want to write papers for conferences or articles for publication. Essay writing trains you for these activities; the processes are just the same. If you keep the needs of your reader in mind, you will be able to write for all occasions.

FURTHER READING

Crème, P. and Lea, M. (2001), *Writing at University: A Guide for Students*, Buckingham: Open University Press. This is a very approachable general introduction to university writing.

Greetham, B. (2001), *How to Write Better Essays*, Basingstoke: Palgrave. An accessible account of how to improve essay-writing techniques.

Peck, J. and Coyle, M. (1999), *The Student's Guide to Writing: Grammar, Punctuation and Spellin*, Basingstoke: Palgrave. This guide provides useful help with the mechanics of writing.

Redman, P. (2001), *Good Essay Writing: A Social Sciences Guide*, London: Sage. Redman presents an excellent guide to all stages of essay writing, including two example essays with a full commentary on their strengths and weaknesses.

Rose, J. (2001), *The Mature Student's Guide to Writing*, Basingstoke: Palgrave. A reminder of the basics of grammar, punctuation and essay-writing techniques.

15 EXAMINATIONS

ADVANCE PREPARATION

Time management is crucial both before and during exams. It is important to plan and think ahead, keeping on top of work as you go along rather than letting it build up and get out of control. Revision will be much easier if you have planned for it early on by structuring your notes clearly (from lectures, workshops and reading) and making summaries of key points. Awareness of the central themes of the course is important, as you can expect them to be relevant for many of the exam questions. One of the key things is to attend lectures and workshops as they will cover the main issues assessed in exams. Lecturers often drop hints throughout the course and not just in the final revision session, which is another good reason to attend regularly. Try to read at least one thing from the reading list every week and keep notes, including the bibliographic details, so you know where the ideas came from. This will enable you to reference literature in your exam, thereby demonstrating your broader knowledge of the topic.

If you want to do well in your exams, it is not enough to rely only on the information you are given in lectures and workshops. You should aim to show evidence that you have done wider reading in relation to each topic. In exams, as in essays, you are expected to reference the texts that you have read when you use ideas from them as evidence for the points you are making. Also bear in mind that examiners are not daft and they know what information you get in lectures and can easily recognise when you are merely repeating this in an essay or in an exam. So do not expect to get a good mark if you just rely on lecture notes and nothing else.

REVISION

Ideally a consistent level of reading (accompanied with clear note-taking) throughout the course will place you in a good position for exam revision – you will also enjoy your course more. Your revision, which should begin at least two or three weeks before the exam, is based on your notes from lectures, workshops and your own wider reading. Having a good grasp of the key concepts and main themes of the course as a whole will enable you to tackle individual questions. These should be highlighted in the introductory and concluding lectures of the course as well as indicated in a section on aims and objectives and/or learning outcomes in the course outline.

For example, in first-year sociology courses, the main kinds of issues you are introduced to are similar to those discussed in Parts II and III of this book, including:

- *The sociological perspective*: questioning taken-for-granted assumptions, seeking social explanations for particular issues

- *Social constructions*: the ways in which we understand the social world changes over time and place (i.e. through history and in different cultures)

- *Definitions of key sociological concepts*: such as power, inequality, marginalisation, identity, class, gender

- *Contemporary social change*: the relationship between sociology and the modern world

- *Agency and structure*: individual action versus institutional structures

- *Methodology*: relationship between theory, data and analysis; key sociological research methods: surveys, interviewing and participant observation.

Consider the ways in which the key themes of your course relate to the different topics which you have studied and think about specific examples you could use to illustrate such points. Some exam questions may require you to draw on evidence from two or three different cultures. Consequently, try to ensure you are aware of several case studies which you could use to back up your arguments. If you are asked to refer to a case study or empirical example, this means that you would need to mention sociological texts which present the findings of research rather than referring to a more theoretical text.

Choosing what to revise

Begin your revision by reading through all your lecture and workshop notes to make sure you have a broad understanding of the course as a whole. Then choose which topics you will study in depth. Instead of planning to do one topic to death before going on to the next, aim to revise all your exam question topics once and then revise them all again, and again. That way, everything gets a fair turn and nothing gets overlooked.

By looking at past papers or asking your tutor, find out how many questions are on the exam paper and how many you are expected to answer. Do all the topics appear every year and how many do you need to revise? What kinds of questions are asked? Is there a particular format, such as you have to answer one question from section A and one from section B? This strategy is sometimes used to encourage you to revise more broadly rather than focus on isolated parts of the course. There may well be some topics that you find easier or more absorbing than others, so these are the ones to concentrate on. Just make sure that, if you are question spotting, you cover a safe amount of material. Students should bear in mind that some questions can be harder than others: some are broad and flexible, others are narrow and specific. It is a good idea to have at least one, and preferably two, spare topics in the bank in case one of your chosen subjects does not come up or the question is asked in a way you do not like.

For each topic you choose to revise, ask yourself the following key question: what is the sociological perspective in relation to this issue? Furthermore, for each of your revision topics, make sure you are familiar with the main sociological arguments, definitions of key terms, central concepts, key sociologists and the most relevant social theories (see example below). Try to ensure that you know of at least three authors who have written in relation to that topic and be familiar with their main arguments and key points so that you can refer to their work by name of author and year of publication in the exam.

Try to revise central issues rather than focus on minor aspects of particular topics. Concentrate on the main sociological questions and concepts that have been explored throughout your course. Revise constructively – do not just spend too much time reading without structuring your notes. Think of ways to remember the important things you are reading about. For example, make notes and write summary lists of the main arguments put forward by different sociologists in relation to each topic. Try making notes of your notes and notes of the notes of your notes until you are down to a postcard's worth or less for each question. Then, check that you can expand it all again to exam-answer size. A glance at these notes before you go into the exam will give you some confidence.

Example of organising revision notes

Course: Social Differentiation

Key topic: Gender

Key themes of the course in relation to gender as a form of social division:
- the social construction of gender (the ways our understanding of gender varies both historically and culturally)

- changes and continuities in relation to gender relations in contemporary Britain
- the relationship between gender identities and social inequalities
- the ways in which gender expectations constrain the behaviour of women or men in different cultures

Definitions: sex, gender, sexism, gender role, gender order, femininity, masculinity

Key concepts: feminism, patriarchy, ideology, socialisation

Social theories: feminist theories including Marxist, liberal and radical approaches

Key sociologists: Connell, Oakley, Walby

Empirical examples: gender and work roles (for example, horizontal and vertical segregation); division of labour in both public and private spheres; gender and education

Cross-cultural examples: including case studies from developing countries, such as Mead's work on gender roles in African societies, Evans-Pritchard's research on the Nuer

Practising exam answers

Examine the kinds of questions that you discuss in your workshops as these are often a good indication of the style and standard of questions which may be asked in the exam. Look at past papers and think how you would manipulate what you know to fit the different ways the questions are worded. Practise planning your response to various questions: write a detailed plan of how you would construct an answer including the key points and the examples you would use to back up each argument.

It is a really good idea at some point, when you are far

enough on with your revision but well before the examination date, to set yourself a paper under exam conditions. A frequently asked question is 'How much should I write?' and this is the best way to find out. How well can you fit your answers to the time allowed for each question? You should take up all the time allowed, so if you run out of things to say, you will have to go back to the books. Always learn more than you need, to allow for all the things that go straight out of your mind under the stress of the exam.

EXAM TECHNIQUES

As with essay writing, in exams it is not just *what* you know but *how* you write it. The way in which you construct your exam answer is important: making sure it has structure, that your points are relevant, that you directly tackle the question being asked. Writing an exam answer is like a speeded-up process of writing an essay (see Chapter 14). The only exceptions are that a full bibliography is not required (instead references are cited by mentioning the authors and year of publication) and, as it is written more quickly, the ways in which arguments are expressed are not always so eloquent or polished. Nevertheless, exam responses are still expected to be well developed with an introduction, middle and conclusion, whilst showing evidence of critical and analytical thinking, and not just description. Students should bear in mind that there is often not a clear-cut right or wrong answer to the particular question being asked but that it depends on how the response is argued and whether the points made are justified. It is usually the case that there are many different ways of answering a question, but so long as you are transparent in how you are focusing your response and you provide clear evidence for your arguments then you should be okay.

Interpreting exam questions

Try to get into the practice of interpreting exam questions (and an essay for that matter) by deciphering clearly what they are asking you to do (see section on 'Planning' in Chapter 14). Read the questions slowly and carefully because many marks can be lost by answering the question you hoped you would be asked rather than the question that is there. Begin by looking for key phrases that you will need to define in your introduction. Then ask yourself, what is the action word of the question? Is it asking what, why, how, evaluate, compare and contrast? When you see the word 'discuss' always read as 'critically discuss' because such a question usually requires you to think critically about different perspectives and often implies that there are at least two sides of an argument which need to be considered. If so, you should present the advantages and disadvantages of different viewpoints, and then evaluate which you think is the most suitable explanation for that particular issue.

Does the question just ask you to explore one issue or does it have two parts to it? Be especially wary of this as you may be in danger of throwing away a good grade by only answering half of the question. Is the question asking you to provide specific examples and can you do that? If you only have one case study which you could refer to and it asks for two, perhaps it is better to tackle a different question. However, stop and think first; do not panic. Maybe you know about one example in detail, but perhaps you could at least briefly mention another and if you feel you know the question well enough, then maybe you would still be able to do it. Nevertheless, if the question asks for three examples, do make sure you refer to three. If it says 'compare and contrast' then do not just discuss the similarities whilst overlooking the differences. The key thing is to make sure you know what the question is getting at before you just dive in and start answering it. Take your time both to read and think about the question. Sometimes it may not appear as if your topic is there, but are you sure? Read the questions

again and double-check before you dismiss that topic and
head for another one.

Example: What is the following question asking you to do?

*What distinctive features can you identify about men and
women's work in Britain? How would you explain changes and
continuities in employment patterns in recent years?*

The first part of the question is relatively straightforward: a 'what'
question which requires you to identify the features of British men
and women's work. The second part of the question asks you not
only to comment on whether these features are new (changes) or
old (continuities), but the key action word is to 'explain' them. This
is an actual example of an exam question and most of the students
who responded to it must have read: 'Do these features reflect
changes or continuities' rather than realising that they had to offer
explanations. Thus many students provided a poor answer by
merely describing the changes and continuities in work patterns,
rather than explaining them. This was not a question about 'how'
patterns have changed, but 'why'. By carefully scrutinising the
wording of the question, mistakes like this can be avoided.

Timing and planning

First, do not be late and do not leave early. The length of time
allocated to an exam reflects the amount of time needed to
answer the questions fully. If you have forty-five minutes to
answer one question, but you have completed it in fifteen
minutes then you will not have provided an adequate response. Use *all* the exam time and if you have some spare
time at the end, read through your answers and make correc-
tions or add some extra points.

Please do not ignore this next piece of advice: spend an
equal amount of time on each question. This may sound

obvious, but it is amazing how many students make a mess of exams because they do not do this. Make sure you know how much time to dedicate to each question and stick as closely as you can to it. Timing is key to writing balanced answers and raising the likelihood of a better overall mark. As you write an exam answer, you pick up marks very rapidly in the first ten or fifteen minutes of writing. After that, the rate at which you collect marks slows down and eventually you reach a plateau. There may even come a point when you end up exposing your ignorance instead of showing off your knowledge and your marks could begin to drop. So, obviously, it is better to begin three questions than to finish two and leave one unstarted.

Work out how much time you can have for each question. Remember to allow for the time it takes to put your name on the paper and to fill in the other administrative details, question-reading time, thinking time and writing an essay plan. Note the time at which you must start to draw each question to a close. Even if you have not completely finished when your time is up, move ruthlessly on to the next question. You may have time to go back and finish it later. Usually, each answer is written in a separate book, but, if this is not the case, leave a big space between answers so that you can go back and add any necessary finishing touches. There is really no point in writing one excellent answer and one very poor one as there are only so many marks to be gained for each response. It is easier to attain a higher mark by writing two good answers rather than one very good and one poor.

You should spend five minutes planning your answer carefully, as it will greatly improve the quality of your response. In your plan you should not only think about what content to include, but also how best to organise it and structure it in a relatively logical way. Write your plan in the exam booklet as it can enable examiners to see whether you are on the right track if you run out of time. Try to write clearly, which is hard when writing quickly. It is crucial that your answer can be easily read by the examiner. However, do not waste time by doing your best writing, as you need to communicate your ideas on paper relatively quickly. Obviously, quality is more important than quantity, but generally about three sides of A4 would be expected for a forty-five minute exam essay (depending also on the size of writing of course). As a whole, students who write four to five sides tend to get higher marks for writing a fuller answer, so long as what they are writing is of good quality and is directly relevant to the question being asked. A student would be struggling to scrape a pass if they wrote less than a page for one answer. However, even if you are really running out of time, never submit absolutely nothing for one question. At the very least, spend five minutes scribbling down an essay plan and a paragraph or two which will gain you some marks rather than zero. Even when you fail an exam question (or essay) you still get some marks which contribute to your overall grade, but getting a zero for not handing in anything for a particular question really penalises your final mark.

Content: building arguments and providing evidence

Attempt to incorporate sociological theories and key sociological concepts in your answers as a way of explaining your response to the specific question. Try not to forget to cover a main aspect of the question but do not worry about trying to include absolutely everything. Focus your response down to four or five key issues and argue them well, backing up your points with empirical examples from sociological research and introducing relevant theories wherever possible. As long as you have answered the question fully, it does not matter if you have left out one or two additional issues.

Remember that examiners are not trying to catch you out and exam questions are usually designed as an opportunity for you to demonstrate what you know. However, it is not all about memorising lots of information, but it is about how you use the information to answer the question that is asked. Ensure that you tailor your knowledge to the particular question and that you argue your points clearly. Students who receive better grades indicate that they have a clear understanding of different sociological debates. They show an awareness that sociology, like the social world, is not clear cut and their exam responses reflect these complexities and shades of grey, rather than writing as if everything were black and white. Also, you should back up arguments with examples drawn from the wider literature. Weaker students tend to rely more on lecture notes rather than showing evidence of broader reading, or they are more likely to describe different empirical studies in turn rather than using them as evidence for the points they are raising.

One of the key difficulties for students under the time pressure of exams is making sure they are being relevant and answering the question directly. The likelihood of losing exam marks for irrelevance should not be underestimated. When constructing your plan in the first five minutes, check that all your points do relate clearly to the question being asked. If they do not, either make sure you can tie them into the question in a relevant way, or think of another point. Explicitly answer the question that has been set rather than just indiscriminately write everything you know on that topic. Relevance is key to ensuring a good exam answer.

If you find yourself writing about something that has not been discussed on your course, then this should raise you to question its relevance. Particularly if you start waffling and writing off the top of your head without really thinking it through. You may find yourself drifting away from a socio-logical perspective into commonsense explanations. Remember, you need to provide evidence for the points you make by referencing the literature, and your points should be well argued rather than merely descriptive. Avoid using anecdotes or personal experience and stick to using sociological evidence and arguments. Similarly, if you realise that you are just repeating essay material, it may mean that you have gone off at a tangent as exam questions are usually intentionally different from assessed essay questions.

Style: clarity and structure

Bearing in mind you are writing under exam conditions, examiners appreciate that the style of your responses will not be as perfectly organised as your essays. Nevertheless, markers do still expect students' ideas to be coherent and to show some kind of logical organisation to the points they are making. In particular, they should see evidence that students have planned their answer and that there is a clear beginning, middle and end, even if the introduction and conclusion are relatively short (usually just one paragraph each). It is important that you are explicit about how each point directly links to answering the question that is being asked. State your arguments clearly and directly: try not to just imply certain things and leave the examiner to read in between the lines. You should still write in a formal style, even though sentences may not always be elegantly expressed. Thus, although you should not waste time thinking over particular words, you should avoid slipping into slang or 'chatty' writing.

> **Introduction:** In the introduction you should demonstrate that you understand the question and set up how you will go about answering it. Hence, your introduction should indicate how you interpret the question and how you will focus it. If it is quite a broad question, you will not be able to cover all aspects so you should say what you have chosen to concentrate on and why. It is useful if you can also acknowledge any wider issues that are involved, even if you will not discuss them in detail in your response. As with essays, there are usually many different ways of tackling an exam question and, providing you cover the different parts of the question, it is your choice how to focus it. So long as you are answering the question, it is up to you whether you take a broad or a more in-depth approach. For example, in your introduction you may need to mention a range of perspectives or issues, even though your exam essay may focus more on just one or two of these. You may also need to briefly

define key terms in your introductory or second paragraph.

Middle of the essay: Ideally you will have planned how
to structure your arguments, striving to make one point,
expand it, back it up with an example and then link into
the next point. Try not to jumble lots of ideas up together
but to some extent, as you are writing under time
pressure, there may be some jumping around from one
point to another and back again.

Conclusion: Sum up very briefly your key points and link
them back to the question. Clearly state where you stand
in relation to the question. Ensure that your conclusion
directly answers the question, such as by evaluating to
what extent you agree or disagree with it, or what the key
issues involved are.

Referencing in exams

As well as drawing on material from lectures and workshop
discussions, in order to get a good mark, you will also need to
show evidence of wider reading. For each topic, aim to be able
to reference *at least* three key texts in the answer you write.
Where possible cite the author and the year of publication
(though do not worry too much if you cannot remember the
exact year) but do not bother to write a full bibliography at the
end. Better exam essays will show a range of reading, drawing
on a variety of sources of empirical research. You would be
unlikely to get a good mark if no references are mentioned,
even if your response is very well written and coherently
argued.

   Good exam essays tend to reference more often and more
accurately than those which receive lower grades. Rather
than just writing 'In India . . .', it is more appropriate if
you can refer to the author of the research: 'In Vatuk's
work on India . . .' You can alternate the style adopted to

mention the literature by introducing authors directly or adding their names after the point is made, as in the following examples:

- Bauman and May (2001) suggest that . . .

- Webster (1990) argues that migration is one of the key features of overurbanisation.

- Migration is one of the key features of overurbanisation (Webster 1990).

Key problems

Overall writing an exam response is like writing an essay, except it is under exam conditions. It is possible to do really badly in an exam essay, if you misread the question or wander off the point. However, you should aim towards improving your exam technique each time and think about where you might have gone wrong and how you could do better next time. Marks are most commonly lost because of:

- Not reading the instructions and doing one question too few or one too many

- Not reading the question and/or failure to understand the question

- Bad time management

- Irrelevance

- Trying to substitute made-up waffle for fact

- Not giving enough examples and/or lack of evidence

- Being too descriptive rather than analytical

- Lack of focus or structure

The best cure for exam nerves is the knowledge that you have studied to the best of your ability. Remind yourself that you are as well prepared as you will ever be, and look forward to showing off what you know. The examiners want you to pass and they are actively looking to reward you for displaying relevant knowledge.

After the exam, it is worth reflecting on your exam performance and making sure that in future exams you continue to do what seemed to work well and improve on any areas of weakness. Remember that there are many other study guides which offer tips for developing your exam techniques which you may like to consult (for example Cottrell 1999; McIlroy 2003). Perhaps you can perceive exams (and essays) as an interesting challenge rather than a huge ordeal – this is probably wishful thinking but it is worth a try!

APPENDIX : GOOD AND BAD EXAMPLES OF ESSAY WRITING

Essay title: *Age is a form of social discrimination. Discuss in relation to children or older people.*

First, deconstruct the question. Try to think through the following points for yourself before reading our suggestions:

1. Ask yourself, what is the action word of this essay title (i.e. what is it asking you to do)?

2. Which key terms used in the title might you need to define in your introduction?

3. How might you focus this essay and why?

1. The action word here is 'discuss' – remember to read '*critically* discuss' (see Chapter 15). Are there two sides to this argument which need to be considered? For example, is age always a form of social discrimination or can it sometimes be experienced positively?

2. Early on in your essay you will need to define 'social discrimination', as this is the key term which should be discussed.

3. Make sure you focus on *either* children *or* older people and not both as the question only requires you to discuss one age group. You may acknowledge briefly that both groups can be discriminated against but then indicate how you made your decision to focus on one of them.
   Read the following 'good' examples of an introduction,

main point and conclusion. Try to scrutinise each paragraph and decide for yourself what makes this a good piece of work before reading our commentary.

EXAMPLE OF A 'GOOD' ESSAY

Introduction:

Age, although a relatively new subject of social study, is a way of differentiating people in society which can be experienced in both positive and negative ways. People at any stage in the life course can be discriminated against because of their age. Social discrimination can be defined as negative treatment that denies 'to the members of a particular group, resources or rewards which can be obtained by others' (Giddens 2001: 687). This essay focuses on the discrimination of older people mainly in relation to the UK. More than 15 per cent of the UK's population currently consists of over 65-year-olds and this ageing population is often referred to as the 'greying' of society (Giddens 2001: 163). Thus, it could be argued that older people now face discriminatory treatment more than ever. First, the essay will examine the impact of retirement followed by the workplace as main factors in discrimination against older people. Subsequently, by drawing on case studies from India and the UK, it explores the ways in which popular discourse can be used to treat older people both positively and negatively. Finally the essay considers how gender and age interact to result in older women's experiences of double discrimination.

Commentary:

This is a very good introduction which begins with a general introductory comment about age to set the scene and show a broad understanding of the topic. Next it defines the key term of the essay question before justifying why it has chosen to focus on older people. The essay's structure is then clearly established enabling the reader to know that four key points will be considered in turn: retirement, work, popular discourse and the intersection of gender and age.

Main section: example of a main point being developed in relation to the theme of retirement:

Retirement contributes to the negative attitudes towards older people as it is generally socially imposed at a particular chronological age, regardless of individual competencies. For example, in the UK the age of retirement at 65 for men and 60 for women is an arbitrary age which 'bears no relationship to the nature of the individual's personality, vitality, biological condition and mental acuity' (Holmes and Holmes 1995: 53). There is no particular decline in physical or mental abilities at this chronological age, and many older people can still be both mentally and physically capable at 60 or 65. However, the notion of the pensioner, the retired older person who receives a pension, tends to be how many older people become defined and this can hide their individual identity. Nowadays, in the UK, retirement is too often deemed to be the gateway to old age (Gatherer 1981: 43) and as a consequence older people become labelled as 'poor and useless' (Vincent 2000: 150).

As we have seen, older people in the UK are often perceived as a homogenous group of 'pensioners' (Phillipson 1998). They are frequently portrayed as a burden to society because of their social and economic dependence on others. Retirement results in a loss of income which can lead to a limited access to certain resources such as housing and car ownership. Giddens (2001: 165) argues that a lack of car ownership restricts access to healthcare, shopping and contact with others, which may affect older people's ability to participate fully in society. Being excluded from the world of work can also reduce older people's social networks and opportunities for engaging in social activities. Therefore, retirement contributes to the discrimination of older people not only by labelling them as a burden but also by restricting their access to social and economic resources that are more readily available to other age groups.

Commentary:

This example illustrates how argument and evidence should be effectively linked. Paragraph one makes the point that retirement forces people to be defined as 'old' whether this reflects their individual circumstances or not. The example of the UK is given backed up by evidence from sociological literature on ageing. The point is developed to show how this leads to older people being labelled in negative terms.

The theme of retirement is expanded in paragraph two by indicating that it can lead to both economic and social exclusion. Notice that the first sentence of paragraph two links back to the previous paragraph to show the connection between the points being made. An example of limited access to resources is provided from Giddens. This point about economic marginalisation is then developed by linking it to social exclusion. The final sentence of the paragraph sums up the main point and directly relates it back to the essay question.

Conclusion:

In summary, this essay has shown that retirement is often forced upon older people, thereby marginalising them from both the social and economic opportunities associated with working. In the workplace older people are frequently devalued and perceived to be less competent than younger workers. A comparison of popular discourse used to refer to older people in the UK and India indicated that social attitudes towards the ageing process are not fixed and vary in different cultures. It was also argued that older women suffer greater levels of discrimination than older men because they can experience both sexism and ageism, particularly through lower levels of pensions and the more negative use of language directed at them. Hence, this essay concludes that age is indeed a form of social discrimination in relation to older people in the UK but that other cultures do not necessarily experience and interpret age in the same way. Therefore, age is a social construction which varies according to time and place, so the extent to which age is a form of social discrimination will also vary through history and in different cultures.

Commentary:
This is a very good conclusion which begins by concisely summarising each of the four key points that were developed in the essay. It then directly states how it answers the question (by agreeing that age is a form of social discrimination in the UK but not necessarily in other societies). Finally, it draws all these ideas together to make a final point in relation to the social construction of age and discrimination.

Please note that this essay title could have been answered in many different ways. The example here focused on retirement, work, language and gender, but a range of other themes could have been addressed such as leisure, the family, division of labour, politics, religion, health, or education. The essay above chose to focus mainly on evidence from the UK with one additional empirical example from India, but this comparison could have run throughout all four of the main points. Alternatively for each of the four points a different society could have been used each time to provide illustrations of the issue. A historical approach could also have been included by using examples from the past to show how our understanding of discrimination changes over time. It does not matter which approach is chosen, providing that it is outlined and justified in the introduction to the essay.

EXAMPLE OF A 'BAD' ESSAY

Introduction:
Within society there are many ways in which individuals and groups are discriminated against. Discrimination takes place where people are socially excluded and treated as though they are unequal. Social discrimination is created and maintained as part of society today because of the negative stereotypes that are connected to people. People can be discriminated against on the basis of their class, sex, ethnicity, disability, age and religion. Ageism, racism and sexism are all types of social discrimination. In all cultures, age is used as a way of differentiating people (Payne, John A. Vincent 2000). Society has

*many social constructs that decide how collective life is
organised. Within every society age is a fixed social construct.
There are three models in trying to define the notion of age,
which are perceived differently from each other, these are
chronological, biological and social.*

Commentary:
The first half of this introduction attempts to set the scene
raising some general points in relation to age. However, these
are poorly expressed and it is not clear that the author fully
understands them. The definition of discrimination is not
referenced to any source. Payne is inadequately referenced
and there is no page number to indicate the exact source of the
idea. The sentence: 'Within every society age is a fixed social
construct' is unexplained and contradictory since social constructions are not 'fixed'. Thus, the author has not demonstrated a clear understanding of what the essay title really
entails. The introduction ends by describing different interpretations of age but this is not made at all relevant to social
discrimination which should be the focus of the essay. The
structure of the essay is not outlined and we do not know
whether childhood or older age will be discussed.

Main section:
*Children are socially discriminated against as they are unable
to participate in activities that adults can engage in. Law-
makers have decided that it would be in children's best interest
if they did not learn to drive until they are seventeen as this is a
responsible age, in some parts of America they may have to
wait until twenty-one. The consumption of alcohol has been
restricted to eighteen years as the body is still growing; it is
unsafe and may cause serious problems to fill the young body
with toxins. It is believed that children are unable to make
these decisions for themselves and need politicians too make
laws on their behalf. Nevertheless they are aloud to decide
whether to have children or get married something that
demands a lot more responsibility than drinking alcohol. At
sixteen they can be fully responsible for a child yet society still*

treats them as a child as they can not take part in all activities that some one of eighteen can.

Commentary:
This paragraph is very descriptive and lacks analysis. It makes a series of jumbled-up points (such as limited participation in social activities but responsibility in others, lack of decision-making power, generational inequalities) and consequently the overall aim of the paragraph is unclear. Apart from one example it is not clear which society these statements are referring to: is the reader meant to assume this is about the UK? These descriptive examples should be linked to arguments about the ways in which age is socially constructed rather than merely biologically determined. More importantly, the issues raised must be explicitly related back to the essay question. This essay could have been written with no knowledge of sociology. There is no indication of sociological thinking backed up by empirical examples. In fact, no proper evidence is provided: there are no references to sociological literature and the examples are not sourced. There are also careless typos and punctuation is poor.

Conclusion:
In summary, the notion of social discrimination can be related to many aspects of society. The main issue addressed within this essay was age, in particular childhood. It can be concluded that there are many factors to consider when discussing age particularly the younger generation, these can include family, work and education.

Commentary:
This conclusion is too short and too vague. It merely reminds the reader that the essay has focused on age, and more specifically on childhood, and that the main three themes covered were family, work and education. However, it gives the reader no indication of what the main findings were. There should be a sentence in relation to each of the three themes highlighting the main points that were argued in the essay. The

conclusion needs to be more specific: what are the many aspects of society and what are the many factors to consider when discussing age? More importantly how does all of this relate to the essay question? It is not at all clear whether the author agrees that age is a form of social discrimination or not, only that it is related to many (unspecified) aspects of society.

GLOSSARY

Ageism – social and individual discrimination based on a person's age.

Agency – often contrasted with 'structure', this term refers to human action and the extent to which we can choose to act without constraint.

Anomie – for Émile Durkheim this term referred to a state of normlessness and a lack of regulation throughout society between social norms and individual aspirations and desires.

Bureaucracy – a rigidly hierarchical form of organisation within which operates a system of impersonalised rules which are followed precisely. Max Weber saw this form of organisation as increasingly becoming the norm within modern societies and which typified modernity.

Capitalism – a socio-economic system based on the widespread use of wage labour and the generalised production of commodities sold in the marketplace for a profit.

Class – a social grouping based primarily on economic position. Members of different classes can have widely divergent life chances.

Collective conscience – a term associated with Émile Durkheim which refers to the widespread morals, beliefs and values common to most individuals within a particular society.

Common sense – the knowledge routinely employed by individuals to explain the everyday world and their action within it.

Crime – actions that break the criminal law of particular societies and which can be followed by formal sanctions and punishment.

Culture – the widespread beliefs and values shared by individuals in a society.

Deviance – a general term for actions that subvert what is established as being 'normal' in society.

Disability – a physical or cognitive 'impairment' that can result in social disadvantage and marginalisation due to discriminatory social practices.

Discrimination – the deliberate limiting of the life chances of an individual or group.

Division of labour – the widespread specialisation of tasks and occupations within a society.

Empirical evidence – information we can verify with our senses, which is usually based on social research that has generated data via a range of available methods.

Epistemology – the theory of knowledge and of how we come to know what we know about the world.

Ethnicity – a contested term that places emphasis on a cultural, rather than a biological, basis for group identity.

Ethnography – a detailed study of a particular group, usually carried out through overt or covert observation.

Feminism – a mode of social thought and varied movement of thinkers and activists united by the common goal of improving the situation of women in relation to men.

Functionalism – a theoretical and empirical approach to the study of the social world that seeks to understand the functions that certain social arrangements and actions have for the maintenance of the whole of society, e.g. the tradition of marriage and funerals.

Gemeinschaft and ***Gesellschaft*** – ('community' and 'society') associated with Ferdinand Tonnies, terms that essentially contrast the features of traditional rural societies with more modern complex industrial societies.

Gender – a term that highlights the socially constructed nature of the categories masculinity and femininity.

Globalisation – the growth of social, economic and cultural interdependencies which are taking place at a global level.

Glocalisation – the relation between global, regional and local processes of social, cultural and economic changes.

Hegemony – associated with Antonio Gramsci and relates to the ways in which the ideas and values of a dominant group tend to become the norm throughout society.

Hermeneutics – the science of interpretation which emphasises understanding the part in relation to the whole.

Historical materialism – Karl Marx's theory of social and historical development which places a key role on the ways in which people organise production.

Historical specificity – makes us aware that many social conditions and arrangements undergo change and cannot be assumed to be fixed in time.

Ideal types – a concept that describes something in its purist form and used as a means to investigate the empirical world.

Identity – the way in which groups and individuals understand themselves.

Ideology – a set of beliefs and values that can be used to justify a particular arrangement of social and individual relations.

Indexicality – a term associated with ethnomethodology and asserts that the meaning of actions can only be understood within the context in which they occur.

Industrial society – a society with a particular set of features such as a dependency on wage labour, a detailed division of labour and the rational application of science and technology to production. This is contrasted to a rural and agricultural based society.

Industrialism/industrialisation – a process whereby production is organised on the basis of wage labour, a detailed division of labour and the rational application of science and technology.

Inequality – refers to differences of opportunities and life chances between groups and individuals.

Interaction – see symbolic interactionism.

Labelling theory – analyses the ways in which powerful groups can negatively label the actions of others.

Marginalisation – alerts us to the processes by which individuals and groups can be socially excluded.

Methods – the range of techniques available for conducting research.

Mode of production – Karl Marx's unit of historical categorisation based on the way people organise production.

Modernisation – the process whereby societies move from being agrarian to industrial.

Modernity – an all embracing term that refers to the main features of the modern world and how this is experienced.

Moral entrepreneurs – Howard Becker's term for those individuals who have the power to influence moral agendas and have their definition of events heard over others.

Moral panic – a term associated with Stanley Cohen which describes and analyses the ways in which there is an exaggerated reaction to a particular event or activity.

Nation – a group of individuals that are united by a common culture, language and identity.

Nation-state – a political entity which represents a population within distinct borders.

National identity – an attachment to a nation, for example, understanding yourself as being 'British'. This may be the basis for 'nationalism'.

Participant observation – a research method in which researchers participate, overtly or covertly, in the group or situation they are observing.

Patriarchy – the domination of men over women.

Personal troubles – from C. Wright Mills and distinct from public issues in that it is a problem that is potentially resolvable only by the individual it affects.

Phenomenology – a philosophical approach which focuses on the way people come to understand their world.

Positivism – a position that emphasises a rigorous, empirically based and scientific approach to the development of knowledge.

Post-industrial society – a society that is no longer based on manufacturing where increasingly people work in the service sector and where information technologies and the manipulation of knowledge are crucial.

Post-modernity – the condition of diversity and fragmentation beyond modernity that is seen to be characteristic of modern societies.

Power – basically, the extent to which you can get people to do what you want. The source of social divisions, and a pervasive aspect of society, conceptualisations of power are crucial to sociology.

Public issues – From C. Wright Mills and distinct from personal troubles, referring to a condition or concern that affects large numbers of individuals and is seen to be resolvable through the intervention of the state.

Questionnaire – a research tool in which informants answer a standardised set of, open or closed, questions.

Race – a socially constructed term based on observed physical and cultural differences.

Racism – a belief in the biological differences between 'races', which can result in forms of discrimination and oppression.

Rationality – for Max Weber this was a feature of modern societies and could be understood as the domination of instrumental and calculating approaches to all spheres of social life.

Reflexivity – the constant critical assessment and monitoring of the self and others, argued by some to be a feature of late modern societies.

Risk – a term often used in relation to the experience we have of late modernity. An awareness of risks undermines the previously held faith in social systems and expert knowledge.

Roles – the behaviour expected of particular social positions.

Sample – a selection of individuals from a larger population.

Sampling frame – an accurate list of the total population from which a sample can be randomly selected.

Semi-structured interviews – a form of interview associated with qualitative approaches to research in which the interviewer explores a number of themes and issues.

Sexism – assumptions and prejudices based on gender categories, stereotypes and notions of appropriate roles for men and women.

Sexuality – a term that refers to sexual orientation, desires and identities.

Social construction – relates to the way in which the social world is the result of social processes and can change over time and between different societies.

Social division – the way in which societies are divided into

groupings of individuals who have similar traits and characteristics, and may be disadvantaged in relation to other
groups.

Social facts – Émile Durkheim's term for ways of thinking,
feeling and acting that are collective and can constrain individual behaviour.

Social problem – a social condition that is seen to be undesir-
able and to which there is often a state response, for example,
poverty, unemployment and rising crime levels.

Social structure – social relations and arrangements that often
have a fixed and given nature, for example, rules of appropriate behaviour for men and women.

Socialisation – the process whereby individuals come to learn
the beliefs and behaviour that are seen to be appropriate for a
particular society.

Society – a term commonly used to refer to the totality of
relations within a geographically bounded area, for example
British society.

Sociological imagination – the title of C. Wright Mills' celebrated text and refers to a way of seeing the world sociologically. Centrally, for Wright Mills, this involved
understanding the ways in which the biographies of individuals and history intersected.

Solidarity – refers to that which binds and integrates individuals together and within society. Emile Durkheim contrasted
'mechanical' with 'organic' solidarity.

State, the – a set of institutions at the centre of a geographically
bounded area which is the legitimate source of rule making
and enforcement.

Status – refers to the prestige and power that can be attached
to individuals and groups and can arise from, for example, an
occupation or social position.

Structuralism – a theoretical perspective that analyses social
structures rather than individuals and derives primarily from
the study of language.

Surveys – a key quantitative research method that involves
asking respondents a series of questions via structured interviews or questionnaires.

Symbolic interactionism – a theoretical perspective that focuses on the ways in which humans create meaning through social interaction.

Theory – a way of understanding and explaining events and phenomena in the world.

Validity – the degree to which the claims you make on the basis of a small sample are a true reflection of the total population.

Values – central ideals and beliefs that inform people's actions and can be common throughout a society, for example, the values of 'family life'.

Verstehen – associated with Max Weber and refers to adopting an empathetic understanding and interpretation as part of our explorations of the world.

BIBLIOGRAPHY

Abrams, P. (1982), *Historical Sociology*, Shepton Mallet: Open Books.

Albrow, M. (1999), *Sociology: The Basics*, London: Routledge.

Anderson, R. J., Hughes, J. A. and Sharrock, W. W. (1986), *Philosophy and the Human Sciences*, London: Routledge.

Audi, R. (1998), *Epistemology: A Contemporary Introduction to the Theory of Knowledge*, London: Routledge.

Bauman, Z. (1978), *Hermeneutics and Social Science: Approaches to Understanding*, London: Hutchinson.

Bauman, Z. (1989), *Modernity and the Holocaust*, Cambridge: Polity.

Bauman, Z. (1990), *Thinking Sociologically*, Oxford: Blackwell.

Bauman, Z. (1991), *Modernity and Ambivalence*, Cambridge: Polity.

Bauman, Z. and May, T. (2001), *Thinking Sociologically*, Oxford: Blackwell.

BBC (2001), 'Top firms exclude women directors', *BBC News*, 25 November 2001, accessed September 2004. <http://news.bbc.co.uk/1/hi/business/1673567.stm>

Beck, U. (1992), *Risk Society: Towards a New Modernity*, London: Sage.

Beck, U. (2000), *What is Globalisation?*, Cambridge: Polity.

Becker, H. (1973), *Outsiders: Studies in the Sociology of Deviance*, New York: Free Press.

Bell, D. (1974), *The Coming of Post-industrial Society*, London: Heinemann.

Belsey, C. (2002), *Poststructuralism: A Very Short Introduction*, Oxford: Oxford University Press.

Berger, P. (1970), *An Invitation to Sociology*, Harmondsworth: Middlesex.

Berger, P. and Luckmann, T. (1967), *The Social Construction of Reality*, Harmondsworth: Penguin.

Berger, P. and Kellner, H. (1981), *Sociology Reinterpreted: An Essay on Method and Vocation*, Harmondsworth: Penguin.

Berman, M. (1983), *All That is Solid Melts into Air: The Experience of Modernity*, London: Verso.

Best, S. (2003), *A Beginner's Guide to Social Theory*, London: Sage.

Bilton, T., Bonnet, K., Jones, P., Lawson, T., Skinner, D., Stanworth, M. and Webster, A. (2002), *Introductory Sociology*, 4th edn, Basingstoke: Palgrave Macmillan.

Bocock, R. (1986), *Hegemony*, London: Tavistock.

Bourner, T. and Race, P. (1990), *How to Win as a Part-time Student*, London: Kogan Page.

Bradley, H. (1996), *Fractured Identities: Changing Patterns of Inequality*, Cambridge: Polity.

Braham, P. and Janes, L. (eds) (2002), *Social Differences and Divisions*, Oxford: Blackwell.

Bryman, A. (2001), *Social Research Methods*, Oxford: Oxford University Press.

Bulmer, M. (ed.) (1982), *Social Research Ethics*, London: Macmillan.

Burgess, R. G. (1984), *In the Field: An Introduction to Field Research*, London: Allen and Unwin.

Callinicos, A. (1983), *The Revolutionary Ideas of Karl Marx*, London: Bookmarks.

Callincos, A. (1989), *Against Postmodernism: A Marxist Critique*, Cambridge: Polity.

Cohen, R. and Kennedy, P. (2000), *Global Sociology*, London: Macmillan.

Cohen, S. (2002) [1972], *Folk Devils and Moral Panics: The Creation of the Mods and Rockers*, 3rd edn, London: Routledge.

Cook, D. (1989), *Rich Law, Poor Law: Differential Response to Tax and Supplementary Benefit Fraud*, Milton Keynes: Open University Press.

Cottrell, S. (1999), *The Study Skills Handbook*, Basingstoke: Macmillan.

Craib, I. (1992a), *Anthony Giddens*, London: Routledge.

Craib, I. (1992b), *Modern Social Theory: From Parsons to Habermas*, 2nd edn, London: Harvester Wheatsheaf.

Crème, P. and Lea, M. (2001) *Writing at University: A Guide for Sudents*, Buckingham: Open University Press.

Croall, H. (1998), *Crime and Society in Britain*, London: Longman.

Cuff, E. C., Sharrock, W. W. and Francis, D. W. (1992), *Perspectives in Sociology*, 3rd edn, London: Routledge.

Dixon, B. R., Bouma, G. D. and Atkinson, G. B. J. (1987), *A Handbook of Social Science Research: A Comprehensive and Practical Guide for Students*, Oxford: Oxford University Press.

Durkheim, É. (1970) [1897], *Suicide: A Study in Sociology*, London: Routledge, Kegan and Paul.

Durkheim, É. (1982) [1895], *The Rules of Sociological Method: And Selected Texts on Sociology and its Method*, London: Macmillan.

Durkheim, É. (1984) [1893], *The Division of Labour in Society*, London: Macmillan.

Eisenstadt, S. (1956), *From Generation to Generation: Age Groups and Social Structure*, New York: Free Press.

Fattah, E. A. (1997), *Criminology, Past, Present and Future: A Critical Overview*, London: Macmillan.

Fetterman, D. (1989), *Ethnography: Step by Step*, London: Sage.

Foucault, M. (1992), *Discipline and Punish: The Birth of the Prison*, Cambridge: Polity Press.

Frisby, D. (1992), *Simmel and Since: Essays on Georg Simmel's Social Theory*, London: Routledge.

Frisby, D. and Featherstone, M. (eds) (1997), *Simmel on Culture*, London: Sage.

Frisby, D. and Sayer, D. (1986), *Society*, Tavistock: London.

Frobel, F., Heinrichs, J. and Kreye, O. (1980), *The New International Division of Labour: Structural Unemployment in Industrialised Countries and Industrialisation in Developing Countries*, New York: Cambridge University Press.

Fulcher, J. and Scott, J. (2003), *Sociology*, 2nd edn, Oxford: Oxford University Press.

Garfinkel, H. (1967), *Studies in Ethnomethodology*, London: Prentice Hall.

Garfinkel, H. (2004), *Harold Garfinkel, Department of Sociology*, Los Angeles: University of California, accessed October 2004. <http://www.soc.ucla.edu/faculty.php?lid=1308&display_one=1>

Giddens, A. (1971), *Capitalism and Modern Social Theory: An Analysis of the Writings of Marx, Durkheim and Max Weber*, London: Cambridge University Press.

Giddens, A. (1972), *Selected Writings*, Cambridge: Cambridge University Press.

Giddens, A. (1976), *New Rules of Sociological Method*, London: Hutchinson.

Giddens, A. (1990), *The Consequences of Modernity*, Cambridge: Polity.

Giddens, A. (1999), *Frequently Asked Questions: Risk Society,* London: London School of Economics, updated November 1999, accessed October 2004. <http://www.lse.ac.uk/Giddens/FAQs.htm#RiskQ1>

Giddens, A. (2001), *Sociology*, 4th edn, London: Polity.

Gilbert, N. (ed.) (1993), *Researching Social Life*, London: Sage.

Goffman, E. (1961), *Asylums: Essays on the Social Situation of Mental Patients and Other Inmates*, London: Penguin.

Goffman, E. (1963), *Stigma: Notes on the Management of a Spoiled Identity*, Englewood Cliffs: Prentice Hall.

Gold, R. (1958), 'Roles in Sociological Field Observation', *Social Forces*, 36: 217–23.

Gowers, E. (1987), *The Complete Plain Words*, Harmondsworth: Penguin.

Gray, K. (2003), 'Sociology: Main Areas of Employment', *Graduate Prospects*, University of Edinburgh, updated January 2003. <http://www.prospects. ac.uk/cms/ShowPage/Home-page/Options-with-your-subject/Your-degree-in-Sociology/Main-areas-of-employment/p!epjejl>

Greetham, B. (2001), *How to Write Better Essays*, Basingstoke: Palgrave.

Hall, S., Critcher, C., Jefferson, T., Clarke, J. and Robert, B. (1978), *Policing the Crisis: Mugging, the State, and Law and Order*, London: Macmillan.

Hall, S. and du Gay, P. (eds) (1996), *Questions of Cultural Identity*, London: Sage.

Hall, S., Held, D. and McGrew, T. (eds) (1992), *Modernity and its Futures*, Cambridge: Polity.

Hammersley, M. and Atkinson, P. (1995), *Ethnography: Principles in Practice*, London: Routledge.

Held, D. and McGrew, A. (eds) (2000), *The Global Transformation Reader: An Introduction to the Globalization Debate*, Cambridge: Polity.

Hetherington, K. (2000), *New Age Travellers: Van Loads of Uproarious Humanity*, London: Cassell.

Hirst, P. and Thompson, G. (1996), *Globalisation in Question: The International Economy and the Possibilities of Governance*, Cambridge: Polity.

Holstein, J. A. and Gubrium, J. F. (1997) 'Active Interviewing', in D. Silverman (ed.), *Qualitative Research: Theory, Method and Practice*, London: Sage, pp. 113–29.

Homan, R. (1991), *The Ethics of Social Research*, London: Longman.

hooks, b. (1986), *Ain't I a Woman: Black Women and Feminism*, London: Pluto Press.

Hughes, J. A., Martin, P. J. and Sharrock, W. W. (1995), *Understanding Classical Sociology: Mark, Weber and Durkheim*, London: Sage.

Jackson, S. and Scott, S. (1996), *Feminism and Sexuality: A Reader*, Edinburgh: Edinburgh University Press.

Jamrozik, J. and Nocella, L. (1998), *The Sociology of Social Problems: Theoretical Perspectives and Methods of Intervention*, Cambridge: Cambridge University Press.

Jenkins, R. (1992), *Pierre Bourdieu*, London: Routledge.

Jenkins, R. (1996), *Social Identity*, London: Routledge.

Jenkins, R, J. (2002), *Foundations of Sociology: Towards a Better Understanding of Human Society*, Basingstoke: Palgrave Macmillan.

Johnson, J. and Bytheway, B. (1993), 'Ageism: Concept and Definition,' in J. Johnson and R. Slater (eds), *Ageing and Later Life*, London: Sage, pp. 200–6.

Kerr, C. (1983), *The Future of Industrial Societies: Convergence or Continued Diversity?*, Cambridge, MA: Harvard University Press.

Kumar, K. (1978), *Prophecy and Progress: The Sociology of Industrial and Post-Industrial Society*, Harmondsworth: Penguin.

Kumar, K. (1995), *From Post-industrial to Post-modern Society: New Theories of the Contemporary World*, Oxford: Blackwell.

Lipietz, A. (1989), *Towards a New Economic order: Postfordism, Ecology and Democracy*, Polity: Cambridge.

Loney, M. with Bocock, R., Clarke, J., Cochrane, A., Peggotty, G. and Wilson, M. (eds) (1991), *The State or the Market: Politics and Welfare in Contemporary Britain*, London: Sage.

Lukes, S. (1974), *Power: A Radical View*, London: Macmillan.

Lyotard, J. F. (1987), *The Post-modern Condition: A Report on Knowledge*, Manchester: Manchester University Press.

Macionis, J. and Plummer, K. (2002), *Sociology: A Global Introduction*, 2nd edn, Harlow: Pearson.

Marsh, I., Eyre, A., Campbell, R., McKenzie, J., Finnegan, T., McIntosh, I., Kilroe, M., Jones, D., Thorogood, N. and Green, J. (2000), *Sociology: Making Sense of Society*, 2nd edn, London: Prentice Hall.

Marshall, G. (ed.) (1998), *The Oxford Dictionary of Sociology*, Oxford: Oxford University Press.

Marshall, L. and Rowland, F. (1998), *A Guide to Learning Independently*, Buckingham: Open University Press.

Marx, K. (1954) [1867], *Capital: A Critique of Political Economy, Volume 1*, London: Lawrence and Wishart.

Marx, K. (1968) [1845], 'The Eleven Theses on Feuerbach', in *Marx and Engels: Selected Works*, London: Lawrence and Wishart, pp. 28–31.

Marx, K. (1975), *Early Writings*, Harmondsworth: Penguin.

Marx, K. (1981) [1894], *Capital: A Critique of Political Economy, Volume 3*, Harmondsworth: Penguin.

Marx, K. and Engels, F. (1968) [1848], 'Manifesto of the Communist Party', in *Marx and Engels: Selected Works*, London: Lawrence and Wishart, pp. 31–63.

May, M., Page, R. and Brunsdon, E. (eds) (2001), *Understanding Social Problems: Issues in Social Policy*, Oxford: Blackwell.

May, T. (1997), *Social Research: Issues, Methods and Process*, Buckingham: Open University Press.

May, T. and Williams, M. (eds) (1998), *Knowing the Social World*, Buckingham: Open University Press.

McIlroy, D. (2003), *Studying @ University: How to be a Successful Student*, London: Sage.

McIntosh, I. (1997), *Classical Sociological Theory: A Reader*, Edinburgh: Edinburgh University Press.

McIntosh, I. (2003a), 'Systems, Fiddling and Strangers: Young People's Understandings of the Welfare state', *Social Policy and Society*, 2 (2): 91–101.

McIntosh, I. (2003b), 'Back to Work?', *Sociology*, 37 (2): 361–6.

McIntosh, I., Sim, D. and Robertson, D. (2004), ' "We Hate the English Except for you, cos you're our Pal': Identification of the "English" in Scotland', *Sociology*, 38 (1): 43–59.

McNeill, P. (1990), *Research Methods*, 2nd edn, London: Routledge.

Mead, G. H. (1934), *Mind, Self and Society*, Chicago: University of Chicago Press.

Miles, S. (2001), *Social Theory in the Real World*, London: Sage.

Moran, D. (2000), *Introduction to Phenomenology*, London: Routledge.

Morgan, P. A. (1985), 'Constructing Images of Deviance: A Look at State Intervention into the Problem of Wife Battery', in N. Johnson (ed.), *Marital Violence*, London: Routledge, pp. 60–77.

Muncie, J. and McLaughlin, E. (eds) (1996), *The Problem of Crime*, London: Sage.

NUS (2004), 'Discrimination: The UK Facts', *The Student Movement in Northern Ireland*, NIStudents.org, updated February 2004 accessed September 2004, <http://www.nistudents.org/sections/community_relations/000449.php>

Oakley, A. (1974), *Housewife*, London: Penguin.

Offe, C. (1985), *Disorganised Capitalism*, Cambridge: Polity.

Outhwaite, W. and Bottomore, T. (eds), (1994), *The Blackwell Dictionary of Twentieth-century Social Thought*, Oxford: Blackwell.

Parsons, T. (1937), *The Structure of Social Action: A Study in Social Theory with Special Reference to a Group of Recent European Writers*, New York: The Free Press.

Payne, G. (2000a), 'An Introduction to Social Divisions', in G. Payne (ed.), *Social Divisions*, London: Macmillan, pp. 1–19.

Payne, G. (2000b), 'Social Divisions and Social Cohesion', in G. Payne (ed.), *Social Divisions*, London: Macmillan, pp. 242–50.

Pearson, G. (1983), *Hooligan: A History of Respectable Fears*, London: Macmillan.

Peck, J. and Coyle, M. (1999), *The Student's Guide to Writing: Grammar, Punctuation and Spelling*, Basingstoke: Palgrave.

Peet, R. (1991), *Global Capitalism: Theories of Societal Development*, London: Routledge.

Plummer, K. (1996), 'Symbolic Interactionism in the Twentieth Century: The Rise of

Empirical Social Theory', in B. S. Turner (ed.), *The Blackwell Companion to Social Theory*, Oxford: Blackwell, pp. 223–51.

Punch, M. (1986), *The Politics and Ethics of Fieldwork*, Beverley Hills: Sage.

Punch, S. (2002), 'Interviewing Strategies with Young People: The "Secret Box", Stimulus Material and Task-based Activities', *Children and Society*, 16: 45–56.

Punch, S. (forthcoming 2005), 'Age', in I. Marsh (ed.), *Sociology: Making Sense of Society*, 3rd edn, Harlow: Pearson.

QAA (2000), *QAA Benchmark Statement – Sociology*, Gloucester: Quality Assurance Agency for Higher Education, updated 2000, accessed October 2004. <http://www.qaa.ac.uk/crntwork/benchmark/sociology.pdf>

Ray, L. J. (1999), *Theorising Classical Sociology*, Buckingham: Open University Press.

Redman, P. (2001), *Good Essay Writing: A Social Sciences Guide*, London: Sage.

Reid, I. (1998), *Class in Britain*, Cambridge: Polity.

Rickards, T. (1992), *How to Win as a Mature Student*, London: Kogan Page.

Roberts, I. (2000), 'Smacking', *Child Care, Health and Development*, 26 (4): 259–62.

Robertson, D. and Dearling, A. (2004), *The Practical Guide to Social Welfare Research*, Lyme Regis: Russell House Publishing.

Rose, J. (2001), *The Mature Student's Guide to Writing*, Basingstoke: Palgrave.

Rostow, W. W. (1971), *The Stages of Economic Growth: A Non-communist Manifesto*, London: Cambridge University Press.

Said, E. (1978), *Orientalism*, London: Routledge and Kegan Paul.

Sayer, D. (1991), *Capitalism and Modernity: An Excursus on the Writings of Marx and Weber*, London: Routledge.

Sennet, R. (2004), *Respect: The Formation of Character in a World of Inequality*, London: Penguin.

Sharrock, W. W. (1986), *The Ethnomethodologists*, London: Tavistock Publications.

Simmel, G. (1990) [1900], *The Philosophy of Money*, London: Routledge.

Sklair, L. (2001), *The Transnational Capitalist Class*, Oxford: Blackwell.

Smith, D. E. (1988), *The Everyday World as Problematic: A Feminist Sociology*, Milton Keynes: Open University Press.

Smith, D. E. (1990), *The Conceptual Practices of Power*, Boston: Northeastern University Press.

Smith, J. (2002), *Moralities: How to End the Abuse of Money and Power in the 21st Century*, London: Penguin.

Thompson, E. P. (1978), *The Poverty of Theory and Other Essays*, London: Merlin Press.

Thompson, P. (1989), *The Nature of Work: An Introduction to Debates on the Labour Process*, 2nd edn, London: Macmillan.

Tong, R. (1989), *Feminist Thought: A Comprehensive Introduction*, London: Routledge.

Turner, B. S. (1999), *Classical Sociology*, London: Sage.

Urry, J. (2000), *Sociology Beyond Societies: Mobilities for the 21st Century*, London: Routledge.

Victor, C. (1994), *Old Age in Modern Society: A Textbook of Social Gerontology*, 2nd edn, London: Chapman and Hall.

Vincent, J. (2000), 'Age and Old Age', in G. Payne (ed.), *Social Divisions*, London: Macmillan, pp. 133–51.

Vincent, J. (2003), *Old Age*, London: Routledge.

Walby, S. (1990), *Theorizing Patriarchy*, Oxford: Blackwell.

Wallerstein, I. (1983), *Historical Capitalism with Capitalist Civilization*, London: Verso.

Winship, I. and McNab, A. (2000), *The Student's Guide to the Internet, 2000–2001*, London: Library Association Pulbishing.

Wright Mills, C. (1959), *The Sociological Imagination*, Harmondsworth: Penguin.

INDEX

age, 58, 87, 92, 94–7, 159,
    191–8
ageism, 92, 97, 199
agency, 32–3, 199
anomie, 23, 199

Baudrillard, Jean, 74–5
Beck, Ulrich, 79, 81
Becker, Howard, 103, 110,
    202
Blumer, Herbert, 44
bureaucracy, 24, 199

capitalism, 21, 72, 82, 199
children, 86–8, 92, 94
class, 21, 51, 77, 84, 87, 89,
    199
classical sociology, 19, 69, 99
collective conscience, 109, 199
common sense, 27–8, 46, 186,
    199
Comte, Auguste, 18, 37
covert observation, 63
crime, 6, 24, 100, 106–12, 199
    crime rates, 107, 111–12
culture, 31, 62, 65, 74, 93, 99,
    199

deviance, 24, 106, 200
difference, 75, 78, 79, 84, 87,
    91
differentiation, 93, 97, 192
disability, 88, 94, 98, 200

discrimination, 91, 97, 191–8,
    200
division of labour, 71, 200
Durkheim, Émile, 19, 22–4, 41,
    42, 103, 110, 199, 204

empiricism, 37–8
employment, 74, 78, 80, 88,
    183
employment opportunities, 12–
    13
Enlightenment, 18–19, 23
epistemology, 56–7, 200
essays, 4, 28, 123–4, 128, 130,
    132, 134, 136, 144, 149–
    75, 191–8
ethnicity, 58, 84, 200
ethnography, 62–5, 69, 200
ethnomethodology, 36, 45–8
examinations, 136, 141, 176–
    90

family, 6, 104
feminism, 50–2, 92, 200
folk devil, 105
Foucault, Michel, 49–50
functionalism, 36, 41–3, 200

Garfinkel, Harold, 28, 44, 45–8
gemeinschaft, 70, 100–1, 200
gender, 30, 51–2, 58, 84, 87,
    89, 179–80, 183, 192–3,
    194, 200